ADVANCE PRAISE FOR *AMAZON GRACE!*

"'To speak of atrocious crimes in mild language is treason to virtue,' Edmund Burke wrote over 200 years ago, and now, as we face mass extinction from the logic of patriarchy, the daring and intense voice of Mary Daly is sorely needed. 'Sin Big!' she challenges (and invites) daring, desperate women everywhere. More impatient and reckless than her previous work, *Amazon Grace* takes the reader on a journey through the horror—and humor—of current environmental/political events, while weaving connections from the herstoric past into the Archaic Future. Foresisters of the past—like Matilda Joslyn Gage—join foresisters of the future to call us to our elemental selves that must emerge for the survival of the planet. Taste these magical words. Feel them. And find the Courage to Sin Big—Here and Now."

—Sally Roesch Wagner, Ph.D., Executive Director,
The Matilda Joslyn Gage Foundation

"The magic of Mary Daly's writings is at work again in this book that overflows with imagination, adventure, genius. Past, present, and future collide, giving form in a most entertaining way to wisdom and hope."

—Marisa Zavalloni, University of Montreal

ADDITIONAL PRAISE FOR MARY DALY'S GROUNDBREAKING BOOKS!

"This latest explosion [*Quintessence*] by the principal progenitor of radical feminism is sure to infuriate those she has already enraged and endear her more deeply to those who will hear within her frantic, fierce—and often funny—manifesto a terrible and timely word. In this highly charged text, she looks back and forward at the same time and issues an urgent summons: 'Biophiliacs unite!' No one who worries about the present direction of genetics and cloning can afford to miss this important book."

—Harvey Cox, author of *Fire from Heaven*

"[The *Wickedary*] succeeds in a way that most books should, but don't; the information it provides is a springboard for the reader, Sparking her to 'dis-coveries' and revelations of her own."

—Julia Penelope, *The Women's Review of Books*

"Daly is an extraordinary woman and [*Pure Lust*] is an extraordinary work.... Her powerful mind, her creative genius, and her uncanny ability to put her finger on the deep emotional, psychological, and spiritual problems are ignored at our peril."

—*The New York Times Book Review*

"A shock of awakening such as is found in the works of Simone de Beauvoir."

—*Publishers Weekly*, on *Gyn/Ecology*

"Important, poetic, and profound...."

—*Booklist*, on *Pure Lust*

"... outrageous and maddening and very smart."

—*Cross Currents*, on *Pure Lust*

"One of the finest minds of our Time."

—*Sojourner*

"Mary Daly is one of the authors whose next book I await as eagerly as the rebirth of Spring."

—Diane Rae Schultz, *Awakened Woman*, on
Quintessence... Realizing the Archaic Future

"Certainly one of the most promising theological statements of our time."

—*The Christian Century*, on *Beyond God the Father*

"This fiery manifesto is recommended for women's studies collections and those readers who are familiar with Daly's previous works and eccentric, exhilarating style."

—*Library Journal*, on *Quintessence... Realizing the Archaic Future*

"I believe Mary Daly has struck the main nerve of the women's movement.... There is a crying need of women for identification with any sort of embodiment of the First Cause, the Female Principle, and Daly's book, *Beyond God the Father*, will be a landmark in that great event which she so perceptively characterizes as the 'second coming—of women.'"

—Elizabeth Gould Davis, author of *The First Sex*

"Daly's insights into the background of radical feminism... are brilliant, and her synthesis of theology, mythology, philosophy, history, and medicine is absolutely overwhelming."

—*Library Journal*, on *Gyn/Ecology*

WELCOME to LOST and FOUND CONTINENT

Sudie Rakusin 2005

Amazon Grace

AMAZON GRACE

RE-CALLING THE COURAGE TO SIN BIG

MARY DALY

palgrave
macmillan

Illustrations © 2005 by Sudie Rakusin

First published 2006 by
PALGRAVE MACMILLAN™
175 Fifth Avenue, New York, N.Y. 10010 and
Houndmills, Basingstoke, Hampshire, England RG21 6XS.
Companies and representatives throughout the world.

PALGRAVE MACMILLAN IS THE GLOBAL ACADEMIC IMPRINT OF
THE PALGRAVE MACMILLAN division of St. Martin's Press, LLC and of
Palgrave Macmillan Ltd. Macmillan® is a registered trademark in the
United States, United Kingdom and other countries. Palgrave is a
registered trademark in the European Union and other countries.

ISBN 1-4039-6853-5 hardback

Library of Congress Cataloging-in-Publication Data
Amazon grace / Mary Daly.
    p.   cm.
Includes bibliographical references and index.
ISBN 1-4039-6853-5
    1. Feminist theory.   2. Ecofeminism.   3. Wild women.
4. Patriarchy.   I. Title.
HQ1190.D34   2006
305.42'09'0511—dc22
                                                        2005048860

A catalogue record for this book is available from the British Library.

Design by Letra Libre, Inc.

10   9   8   7   6   5   4   3   2

Printed in the United States of America

To
ANDREA DWORKIN,
A-MAZING AMAZON
WHO THROUGHOUT HER ENTIRE LIFE AND WORK
DEMONSTRATED THE COURAGE TO SIN BIG

TO MY FAITHFUL FELINE FRIEND, COTTIE,
WHOSE NAME IS DERIVED FROM THE IRISH WORD COT,
MEANING CAT, AND WHOSE
DEEP BACKGROUND NAME IS FEARLESS.
ALSO TO MY FORE-FAMILIAR, AILLE OG
(MEANING IN IRISH "YOUNG BEAUTY"),
WHO FOLLOWED IN THE PAW-STEPS OF
WILD CAT, THE ORIGINAL FORE-FAMILIAR

AND,
AS ALWAYS,
TO MY PARENTS,
ANNA AND FRANK,
WHOSE PRESENCE CONTINUES TO INTENSIFY
IN THE COURSE OF TIME

Contents

Acknowledgments   xv

Introduction
The Challenge of This Book   1

Chapter One
The Desperate Leaping Hope of Radical
Elemental Feminism   5

Chapter Two
Beyond Hopelessness: Extra-ordinary Triviality   11

Chapter Three
The First and Final Cause: She Who Attracts   17

Chapter Four
Realizing the Courage to Hear, Name, and Create Nemesis   31

Chapter Five
What Terrific Shock Will Be Shocking Enough?   43

Chapter Six
Quantum Leaping Ahead/Back to Lost and
Found Continent, 2056 BE (Biophilic Era)   55

Chapter Seven
A Transtemporal Exchange of Information
and Strategic Discussion   65

Chapter Eight
Women's Space and Amazon Grace   79

Chapter Nine
The Self-Destruction of Patriarchy and the
Re-emergence of Female Power   85

Chapter Ten
Seeing Through Phallocracy's Biggest Lies and
Reversing Its Rotten Reversals   99

Chapter Eleven
The Animals—Here and There   115

Chapter Twelve
In the Light of the Brontosaurus   123

Chapter Thirteen
Facing the Current Mass Extinction: Rising to the
Challenge of Re-Claiming Biophilia   131

Chapter Fourteen
Back Again: More on Inclusive Transcendence   143

Chapter Fifteen
A Late-Night Conversation with Matilda   153

Chapter Sixteen
Focusing on the Present Together   165

Chapter Seventeen
Keeping Hell at Bay   181

Chapter Eighteen
The Armageddon Election? The Slide Toward Theocracy   185

Chapter Nineteen
Moving Forward with Thoughts about Tsunamis,
Bushites, and the Theocratic Right   193

Chapter Twenty
A Wider Perspective on Tsunamis   199

Chapter Twenty-One
The Sweetest Word   207

Chapter Twenty-Two
We *Can* Stop It *Now*   225

Notes   233
Index   245

Acknowledgments

MANY FRIENDS OFFERED ENCOURAGING COMMENTS on the manuscript at various stages. Others participated in conversations over
the years that helped to trigger new ideas. The following list of
names does not signify a hierarchical order of importance. Rather
it is more like an interconnecting Web reflecting synchronistic/
Syn-Crone-istic events characteristic of this Time.

I thank Kay Mann, Jane Caputi, Emily Culpepper, Mary Hunt,
Marisa Zavalloni, Roseanne Barr, Betsy Beaven, Betty Farians,
Barbara Hope, Pam McCarron, Annie Lally Milhaven, Lori
Getz, Ann Marie Palmisciano, Ioma Ax, Mary Ellen McCarthy,
Karen O'Malley, Robin Hough, Nancy Kelly, Wendy Stein, Pat
Green, Nelle Morton, Jennifer Rycenga, Mary Lou Shields, Mary
Stockton, Hye Sook Hwang, Sally Roesch Wagner.

For their important work I am thankful to my thoughtful liter-
ary agent Donald Cutler and my gracious editor Amanda Johnson
of Palgrave Macmillan at St. Martin's Press.

Donna Cherry has been a skillful and hardworking production
editor. Barbara Flanagan has been my copy editor *par excellence*—
and indexer as well.

I thank Josie Catoggio for her advice and help with publicity.
Gail Bryan is my creative and painstaking photographer. Sudie
Rakusin's illustrations delightfully enhance the book.

I thank my Foresisters Past, Present, and Future. In fairness and
as usual, I thank my Self and—

Quintessentially Speaking—
I thank Goddess!

THE CHALLENGE OF THIS BOOK

AMAZON GRACE IS A CHALLENGE AND AN INVITATION hurled out to Daring, Desperate Women everywhere. In this malignant time the rulers of patriarchy multiply divisions endlessly. They impose multiple blindfolds/mindfolds upon women, rendering us unable to see the artificially constructed walls that cut us off from our-Selves, each Other, and the natural world. I have Named this state of escalating division *diaspora*, meaning "exile, scattering, migra-tion" (*Webster's*).*

Wild, Wise Women can learn to seize the dreadful diaspora as an Outlandish opportunity. Migrating, Voyaging women can be like stars in an expanding universe. The ever intensifying magnet-ism of seemingly "isolated" women can draw other stars together. Forming New Galaxies of Wonderlusting Cronies, we recognize the imposed diaspora as an occasion for creative communication and transformation. Those who are Realizing a Spark of Magnetic

---

*Webster's Third New International Dictionary of the English Language, hereafter referred to as *Webster's.*

Genius in ourSelves can convert the negative condition of dias-
pora/scattering/exile into our own Expanding Presence. Overcoming the disconnect within and among women is profoundly
related to the project of healing the multileveled fragmentation
(environmental, social, political) inflicted on all inhabitants of this
planet by the lethal disease known as patriarchy. This book is an
invitation to Sin Big! As I explained in *Pure Lust:*

> It is pixilating to find that the word *sin* is probably etymologically
> akin to the Latin *est,* meaning (s)he *is,* and that it is derived from
> the Indo-European root *es-,* meaning *to be* (*American Heritage Dic-
> tionary*). Clearly, our ontological courage, our courage to be, im-
> plies the courage to be WRONG. Elemental be-ing is Sinning; it
> requires the Courage to Sin.[1]

This absolutely necessary process starts Here and Now. As a
work of charting this Journey, *Amazon Grace* organically follows
my earlier work *Quintessence... Realizing the Archaic Future: A
Radical Elemental Feminist Manifesto.**

As Daughter of *Quintessence, Amazon Grace* Springs/Spins off,
carrying threads that were Dis-Covered in that late-twentieth-cen-

---

*Likewise, *Quintessence* flows from all my previous work:
The Church and the Second Sex (New York: Harper and Row, 1968; reissued with
   Autobiographical Preface to the 1975 Edition and Feminist Postchristian In-
   troduction, New York: Harper and Row, 1975; reissued with New Archaic
   Afterwords, Boston: Beacon Press, 1985).
Beyond God the Father: Toward a Philosophy of Women's Liberation (Boston: Bea-
   con Press, 1973; reissued with Original Reintroduction by the Author,
   Boston: Beacon Press, 1985).
Gyn/Ecology: The Metaethics of Radical Feminism (Boston: Beacon Press, 1978;
   reissued with New Intergalactic Introduction by the Author, Boston: Beacon
   Press, 1990).
Pure Lust: Elemental Feminist Philosophy (San Francisco: HarperCollins, 1984;
   London: The Women's Press, 1984; distributed in the US by Trafalgar Square
   Publishing).
Websters' First New Intergalactic Wickedary of the English Language, Conjured in
   Cahoots with Jane Caputi (Boston: Beacon Press, 1987; New York: Harper-
   SanFrancisco, 1994).

tury work and Weaving them differently, elaborating further connections. In order to Hear these connections, it is helpful to READ
OUT LOUD these words. For readers who cannot *Hear* written
words in their heads and feel them as they read, it is especially important to Speak them Out Loud. This is true in the case of poetry
and also in the case of my books. For Words are Elemental *sounds*
and cannot be fully grasped by merely scanning pages of print.

As Sister and Companion to *Quintessence,* this book strives to
be faithful to the Original work, carrying on with the task. It
comes into Be-ing in the twenty-first century a.d. (archetypal
deadtime) as the *foreground* becomes more hideous.[2] *Amazon
Grace* calls forth the deep Background. *Background,* as defined in
the *Wickedary,* is

> the Realm of Wild Reality; the Homeland of women's Selves and
> of all other Others; the Time/Space where auras of plants, planets,
> stars, animals and all Other animate beings connect.[3]

So this book is perhaps even more impatient and restless/reckless
than the parent volume. The strong propensity for Quantum
Leaping may be more desperate and exuberant, but the profound
connections are obvious.

As I wrote in *Quintessence:*

> Journeyers expand our Presence by means of magnetism. We are
> drawn to each other across temporal and spatial divides. Hence
> Expanding Presence is Magnetic Presence, which is experienced
> by many Crones and Cronies as Magnetic Magic.[4]

As a work of creating Biophilic, Magnetic Presence, *Amazon
Grace* carries on this Magical, Elemental tradition. In *Quintessence*

Outercourse: The Be-Dazzling Voyage (New York: HarperSanFrancisco, 1992;
London: The Women's Press, 1993; distributed in the U.S. by Trafalgar
Square Publishing).
*Quintessence . . . Realizing the Archaic Future: A Radical Elemental Feminist Man-
ifesto* (Boston: Beacon Press, 1998).

I explained that Elemental Magnetism includes animal magnetism, that is, a Spiritlike force residing within and emanating from
animals:

> Thus the Expanding Magnetic Presence of Time-Traveling
> Cronies should not be seen as an event isolated from the attrac-
> tive/attracting activities of other Elemental creatures. All partic-
> ipate in the dynamic drawing powers of the *Final Cause,* the
> indwelling, always unfolding goal or purpose perceived as Good
> and attracting one to Act, to Realize her own participation in
> Be-ing.[5]

Consistent with this premise, *Amazon Grace,* like *Quintessence,*
involves Time/Space Travel to Lost and Found Continent, whose
inhabitants—e.g., Kate, Annie, Sophie, Anowa—have escaped archetypal deadtime and live in an Archaic Future, which is rooted
in an Archaic Past.* I know the animals and women on Lost and
Found from my travels there a short time ago. I set out in 1998
and arrived in 2048 BE (Biophilic Era). We are good friends, and
so it is Natural that we visit each other Occasionally. These Foresisters of the Future accept me as a Foresister of their Past. Our
reunions are joyous, thought-provoking, often rowdy. They are astonishing Transtemporal victory celebrations.

---

*These women are among the original inhabitants of Lost and Found Continent.
In particular, Annie added her "Cosmic Comments and Conversations" to *Quintessence* using the name *Anonyma* "in order to honor and signify [her] bonding
with the countless women of the patriarchal era who could not publish under
their own names." The inhabitants of Lost and Found Continent have "reverse[d] the patriarchal reversals and form[ed] a Network Named 'Anonyma'"
(*Quintessence,* p. xi).

CHAPTER ONE

THE DESPERATE LEAPING HOPE OF RADICAL ELEMENTAL FEMINISM

IN THIS CHAPTER I UNDERTAKE AN ANALYSIS of our current experience of Radical Elemental Feminist diaspora, using clues from quantum theory and Aristotelian and Thomistic philosophy.

Seen from a quantum perspective, Dissipation—the process by which energy fades away—can be understood as playing a role in the creation of New Reality. Dissipation is part of a process by which a system lets go of its present form in order to re-emerge in some form(s) better suited to the present environment.

Understood in this context, Radical Elemental Feminism in the twenty-first century can be seen as poised for moving into a phase of increasing efficacy and influence. Women who have suffered losses which are penalties for not selling out can emerge as Memory-bearers of great creative and magnetic power.

Given this possibility, it can be seen that the fantastic explosions of Gynergy[1] in the 1960s, '70s, '80s, and '90s were part of a process of forging new strengths and skills, so that Wild Women of all ages, inspired by our inherited memories of glory, can begin to rise again. Our Movement must re-emerge in forms better suited to the demands of the Present.

The escalation of the takeover by the oppressors of women is worldwide. The new forms that will be assumed by re-emerging Radical Feminism must take into account both the extremity of the atrocious conditions under which many women now struggle to live and the global stealth campaign that often keeps the majority of women—even the majority of feminists—in a smog of unawareness and denial. This involves Daring to Know and Name the ways in which our victories are now being used against us. The Hope that we can do anything about this state of betrayal and reversal requires faith in the "fabric of unseen connectedness."[2] At a level we can't discern, there is an unbroken wholeness, an "implicate order" in which discrete events are united.[3]

Effecting changes in small places—seemingly small changes—is ineffably important, for this enables us to work with the flow within that small system and thus have impact elsewhere. Such changes create large systems change because they participate in an unbroken wholeness.[4]

This is a Newly understood way of moving toward attaining critical mass. Unseen connections make it possible to create effects at a distance. This observation matches a rather ordinary experience. Women sometimes do not share a common language to Name our experiences, but the commonality is recognizable in our descriptions of comparable events in our lives.

The process of coming Home together outside the alien territory of phallocentric institutions is recognized by Wild Women as abrupt, uncomfortable, and unpredictable. Of course, it was always inherently predictable, because this is our natural destiny, our Final Cause. But perhaps it seemed far off and even impossible when we were weakened by the physical, emotional, spiritual toxins of the alien environment foisted upon us as "normal" and balanced.

The snatching away of Wild Women's Space/Spaces—our jobs, our classrooms, our bookstores, our books, the places/times required for Cosmic Conversations—can serve as an incentive for opening the doors to New alignments in Space. Having been thrown off balance, Wild Women can find New opportunities to regain our proprioception—the Sense of where we are in Space, Here and Now. In Other words, we are challenged to Realize our participation in Be-ing in the Widest, Wildest Sense. This happens when we confront and transform the specific circumstances in which we find ourSelves.

The experience of Moving Out—of Leaping off the boundaries of pseudo-secure pseudo-reality—hurls us into touch with the Universe in a deeper way. We reach existential understanding of the truth suggested in the language of quantum physics, that the unseen connectedness makes possible quantum leaps.

To speak about this phenomenon in a different way: Goddess is in her Heaven, that is, Here in the Background, giving us energy for Lusty Leaps beyond dreary constrictions of the phallocratic foreground/flatland. All's right with the Background world, which secretly and mysteriously creates opportunities for Leaping.

This insight arises from the experience of Radical Elemental Feminists who recognize that the Reality which is larger and deeper than patriarchy can transform and use oppressive situations to Reawaken the *X-factor*. I have defined this in *Wickedary* as "the Spring of be-ing; the unpredictable, unpossessable Nature of the Wild, which forever escapes the technocrats, medical and scientific researchers, 'developers,' and other demonic destroyers of living creatures."[5] The X-factor/faculty inspires us to get on with our work/play of creating the Archaic Future. This is our true Future, rooted in the Archaic Past, which transcends the perpetually stagnant state of stagnation and is created by successions of Original Acts/Actions.

THE DEMANDS OF THE TWENTY-FIRST-CENTURY PHYSICAL/SPIRITUAL ENVIRONMENT

A major development in twentieth-century feminism was increasing recognition that the cause of women and the cause of ecology are profoundly interconnected. How could anyone not see this? It is essential to See and Name the fact that the Earth and its inhabitants are now targeted for hideous destruction. Women are Life-Givers. We are targeted by necrophiliacs, and our work is to be Life-Savers, Life-Enhancers.

We are nearer to a global ecological collapse than ever before in human history. One of the few major scientists to be openly critical of the twenty-first-century technologies—genetics, nanotechnologies, and robotics—is Bill Joy, co-founder and former Chief Scientist of Sun Microsystems. Joy describes these technologies as "so powerful that they can spawn whole new classes of accidents and abuses."[6] He states that "we are on the cusp of the further perfection of extreme evil, an evil whose possibility spreads well beyond that which weapons of mass destruction bequeathed to the nation-states, on to a surprising and terrible empowerment of extreme individuals."[7]

These technologies are funded and patented by "great" universities, corporations, and the military, and they are promoted by our lawmakers. What's at stake is "the profound, irreversible alteration of all life on earth, and the proposition that nature has become irrelevant."[8] Francis Fukuyama has stated that "within the next couple of generations we will have definitively finished human history because we will have abolished human beings as such. And then, a new posthuman history will begin."[9]

In his pernicious book *Remaking Eden: How Cloning and Beyond Will Change the Human Family*, Dr. Lee Silver, an advocate of human genetic engineering, argues that in the future, society will be divided into genetic classes—the GenRich 10% of the population—and the other 90%, the "naturals," who have not been genetically improved. Since these genetic changes will become part of the hereditary germline, class divisions will be permanent.[10]

In addition to—but interrelated with—human eugenics, we are confronted with the emergence of nanotechnology. Nanotechnologists attempt to go beyond genetics to the atomic structures of all things. This they plan to do by improving nature, that is, by isolating and re-positioning atoms and molecules into entirely new "products." Dr. Richard Smalley explains that for nanotechnologists everything is subject to re-creation. He and others foresee a time when self-replicating nanomachines will take over the world.[11]

To complete the trinity of technological nightmares there is robotics, i.e., robotic science, which is moving toward a "post-biological" future. A champion of this branch of the approaching brave new world is Dr. Hans Moravec, who in his book *Mind Children* maintains that humans will be able to download the contents of our brains into mobile, autonomous, self-replicating robots. He writes:

> Our culture will then be able to evolve independently of human biology and its limitations, passing instead directly from generation to generation of ever more intelligent machinery.[12]

The horror of the degradation, fragmentation, disintegration that is implied in all of these projects is unfathomable. The "profound, irreversible alteration of all life on earth" that is at stake is apparently impossible for most people to grasp. The walls of denial are thick beyond measure. Indeed it is discouraging to speak about such things and encounter these walls. If we think and speak in ordinary foreground ways, our situation may appear hopeless.

CHAPTER TWO

BEYOND HOPELESSNESS:
EXTRA-ORDINARY TRIVIALITY

BUT WHAT IF WE TRY TO BE-THINK/BE-SPEAK in Extra-ordinary Background Ways? According to *Webster's Second New Intergalactic Wickedary of the English Language* (a text written in the imagination and not yet incarnated in book form) the word *Extra-ordinary* means "very ordinary, Super-naturally ordinary, commonplace. Example: *Trivia.*"[1]

The first materialized *Wickedary* (1987) explains that *Trivia* is derived from the Latin *trivium*, meaning "crossroads." *Trivia* is defined as follows:

> Name of the Triple Goddess, who is commonly encountered at crossroads; Name which conveys the commonplace character of meetings with the Goddess; Name which raises Counterclock Whys, countering the classic patriarchal hierarchical reversal/supposition that sacredness and great value imply scarcity and secrecy, i.e., "mystery."[2]

An important note follows this definition:

The classical figure of Hecate, Goddess of Witches, was often built upon a triangle, with faces turned in three directions. The Hecate statues were set up at the crossing of three roads; hence the name Trivia. Throughout the Middle Ages and even today, crossroads, specifically the places where three roads converge, were/are recognized as loci of Natural visions and happenings.[3]

This idea was further Spelled out by the founding editors of the Radical Feminist journal Named *Trivia: A Journal of Ideas*. As they have written:

> TRIVIA... describes the matrix of our creative power, the gatherings of wise women in which our ideas originate and continue to live.... As we conceive it, TRIVIA is the place where our friendships and our ideas assume their original power and significance.[4]

In such Trivial circumstances something Extra-ordinary can indeed happen.

The Hope that then can arise is Realizing Hope, that is, Hope that inspires us to *Realize,* meaning, "'to make real... bring into concrete existence: ACCOMPLISH ... to bring from potentiality to actuality: ACTUALIZE.... to conceive vividly as real: be fully aware of'—*Webster's:* These definitions have been awarded *Websters'* Intergalactic Seal of Approval."[5]

In the face of the unthinkable hell that the technomaniacs are attempting to manufacture and spread, Hopeful Wild Women can Realize our *Real Presence,* that is, "Female Elemental participation in Powers of Be-ing, which implies Realizing as Present our past and future Selves."[6] It is possible that we can also Realize as Present Other Past and Future Elemental realities.

There are no ordinary/foreground ways to think and speak about this interconnectedness. However, there are Extra-ordinary ways of Be-Thinking and Be-Speaking about it. According to the *Wickedary, Be-Thinking* means

> Re-membering the Original Self; Re-calling Original Questions; thinking the way ever deeper into the Wilderness, the Background.[7]

Be-Speaking means

> 1: Auguring, foretelling, Speaking of what will be 2: bringing about a psychic and/or material change by means of words; speaking into be-ing.[8]

These words Name interconnectedness which involves Transtemporal/Trans-spatial Consciousness, Communication, Sisterhood, Conversations, Synchronicities, Travels. In other words, they signify active participation in the Harmony of the Universe.

Women who are Wild enough to confront the nothingness of the nothing-loving technomaniacs and to Realize our Hope in ourSelves will not feel totally unfamiliar with the interconnectedness of the quantum universe. Nor are we alienated by the thought that, instead of being empty, space has become filled with unseen connections. Indeed, this is our common experience, and it makes possible faith in the worth of our particular works and acts, which have wide-ranging effects.

Wild Women's experiences of unseen connectedness also inspire Fantastic Daring and increasing Self-confidence. As Travelers and Weavers in a participative universe we increasingly trust our own judgment even when our reasons are not evident to others. This progress happens especially when we learn to sense the presence of fields—spatial structures which exert visible, tangible influence, even though they themselves are invisible, intangible, inaudible, tasteless, and odorless.

Rupert Sheldrake's theory of morphogenetic fields can be helpful to Weird Searchers seeking to understand the possibility of emergence of New Forms in desperate times of decay/dissipation, such as the beginning of the twenty-first century. Morphogenetic fields are built up through the accumulated behaviors of species members. After part of a species has learned a behavior, such as bicycle riding, others will find it easier to learn that skill.[9]

Such fields, Sheldrake hypothesizes, "are shaped and stabilized by morphic resonance from previous similar morphic units, which were under the influence of fields of the same kind. They consequently contain a kind of cumulative memory and tend to become increasingly habitual."[10] He defines *morphic resonance* as follows: "The influence of previous structures of activity on subsequent similar structures of activity organized by morphic fields. Through morphic resonance, formative causal influences pass through or across both space and time, and these influences are assumed not to fall off with distance in space or time, but they come only from the past."[11]

WHY WILD WOMEN CAN LAUGH AT THE BACKLASH

Wild Women justifiably Weep, Rage, and Act against the backlash and at the stealth campaign to shut us down. But we are also able to Laugh at it because of our Realizing Hope. I am suggesting that this Hope is rooted in our history and in intuitive certainty of the power of that history to affect the Present, as it passes through and across both space and time. We can boldly assume that through morphic resonance, formative causal influences from our history are with us Now. They contain a kind of Cumulative Memory and tend to become increasingly habitual. The fields and forms from our Archaic Past are Here Now.

These forms reside in the morphogenetic field. We have seen that when individual energy combines with such forms, they pattern behavior without the need for laborious learning of that skill or habit. Not merely bicycle riding but also such skills/habits as writing, organizing, composing music, and practicing Karate and virtues such as Creative Courage are developed by combining individual energy with forms in the morphogenetic field. In this way Radical Elemental Feminist Powers grow and expand. Realizing these Powers is the work of the Sixth Dimension, and it moves by Leaps and Bounds.

According to quantum theory, when an electron jumps from one atomic orbit to another, a whole "system" is creating the conditions that lead to the sudden jump. Wild Women can under-stand that the "system" that creates the conditions leading to our apparently sudden Leaps is larger than the patriarchal system. It is the Universe in which we participate by Realizing who we are that uses and incorporates even the oppressive acts of the patri-archs to promote the creation of the X-factor.

Knowing this context enables Wild Women to understand the backlash. The bosses of bullydom are terrified of our Female En-ergy (Gynergy) and of its potency to combine with the Forms from our Archaic Past, which we can Re-member. Our Cumula-tive Memories are always available to us, and despite all efforts to dis-member us, our desire/determination and capacity to Re-member grows.

Naturally/unnaturally the bullies do not understand such Wild Female power, but they do have cowards' capacity to sense danger and stop at nothing to nip it in the bud. This craven cunning in-cites them to use every means to stunt strong Females. Mindlessly they place innumerable obstacles in the way of Wayward Women. However, whenever/wherever Graceful Amazons persevere, there is Hope that we can succeed in combining our energies with the Forms/Ideas in the morphic fields whose resonance we can so deeply Sense.

This is why they have tried to kill our Memories and Hopes by targeting our books, our bookstores, our publishers, our women-only classrooms, our Radical Feminist classes and conferences, our women's health networks, our women's restaurants, and Other Women's Spaces. But since Wild Women are on to such tricksters' dirty tricks and can understand that they are motivated by onto-logical impotence, we can laugh at them, renew our process of combining Gynergy with Archaic Forms, and, well, Fly.

A major springboard for Flying is Be-Laughing, which is de-fined in the *Wickedary* as follows:

> expression of Elemental humor, carrying Lusty Laughers into the Background: ontological Laughing; be-ing Silly together; Laughing

that cracks man-made pseudo-reality; Laughing that breaks the
Terrible Taboo, Touching the spirits of women, enlivening auras,
awakening Hope.[12]

"Be-ing Silly together" is crucial. The word *Silly* is derived from
the Middle English word *sely* or *silly*. In a truly Wicked sense it
means "Happy, Blessed, Graceful—applied esp. to giggling Gag-
gles of Geese and Gossips."[13]

The Silliness of Wild Women is a manifestation of the unseen
fabric of connectedness. It is a sign of recognition to each Other
that we are not alone in our Seeing, Knowing, Sensing what Is behind the scenes. It is an eruption of the Other Side in Amazon
consciousness. It is a signal that we are Bigger than the backlash.
Naturally we "Sin Big."[14]

Be-Laughing Women Crack Up as we crack the limitations
and boundaries of the foreground world. Instead of feeling like
isolated particles lost in the loneliness of space, Spinsters and
Weavers find ourSelves Spiraling in vibrating Space that is filled
with cosmic connections that are crying out to us to Realize them
Now.

This brings me to the subject of the next chapter—Goddess the
Verb, who is Seen/Unseen as the Hidden Cause, that is, the Final
Cause, who causes by attraction, beckoning us to action.

Chapter Three

The First and Final Cause:
She Who Attracts

THE WRITING THAT FOLLOWS SURGES from an apparently Strange blend of sources: thirteenth-century philosophy/theology, together with late-twentieth- and early-twenty-first-century analyses of impending/already occurring global atrocities. The contemporary analyses can be found in recently published books and journals and—in a less reliable and trustworthy fashion—in ordinary media. My medieval sources are mainly the writings of Thomas Aquinas.

In the face of the devastation already wrought and being planned in this century, Trivial Women can consciously participate in the ongoing weaving of webs of connectedness in the Universe. We do this by diligently following our deep Purpose, that is, our Final Cause.

A brief re-view of the Aristotelian and Thomistic concept of causality is no doubt in order. As I explained in *Beyond God the Father:*

When Aristotle wrote of the "final cause," he intended "cause" to mean that which brings about an effect. Scholastic philosophers followed the Aristotelian theory of the "four causes" to explain change. According to this theory the material cause is that out of which something is made (as the wood in a table). The formal cause is that which determines its nature (as the shape of the wood which makes it a table and not a chair or something else). The efficient cause is the agent that produces the effect by her/his/its action (as the carpenter who produces the table). The final cause is the purpose which starts the whole process in motion (as the goal of having an object upon which to place books, papers, and other items). The final cause is therefore the first cause, since it moves the agent to act upon the matter, bringing forth a new form.[1]

There are more sophisticated examples than this, which reveal the complexity of the theory of the four causes. One need simply ask about the causes of the wood itself to glimpse the difficulties. The point I am stressing here, however, is the absolutely prior and primal role of the Final Cause. As a well-known scholastic axiom states:

> The final cause is the cause of causes, because it is the cause of the causality of all the other causes.[2]

Unfortunately, Aristotle and his followers developed this philosophy within a society that was imprisoned in a static worldview. The role of the efficient cause (agent) was seen as actualizing a potential that was already there and that had already been realized. There was no fully developed idea of evolution, of a Real Future, of an X-factor. There was no Quantum Leap into the Future. The final cause was the source of limited change, but everything was trapped in an ultimately changeless world. For Wild, Wicked Women, Realizing the Final Cause is something utterly Other than this.

THE FINAL CAUSE IN AN INFINITELY SPINNING WORLD

Under the gruesome rule of patriarchy A-mazing Amazons are made to feel that we have lost our senses. We struggle to regain our Sense of Direction. This requires practicing *Space-Craft*. As explained in the *Wickedary:*

> Space-Craft . . . is the art of Spinning beyond the compass. It is also skill in walking/talking the Wrong Way, moving in Wicked directions, opening doors to Other dimensions, Other Spatial perceptions. By reversing the reversals of the snoolish space controllers, we enter a different context. This is Metapatriarchal Space/Time, beyond the measurements of compasses and maps.[3]

For anyone who has retained a Primal Memory of connectedness with the Wild, the thought that she could be severed from this—or that the Wild itself could be destroyed—stirs ineffable feelings of horror. Although such severance and destruction have always been essential to the patriarchal agenda, they have rapidly escalated in recent years.

An atmosphere of such impending evil has become ever more widespread and intense since the mid-1990s. One typical moment of manifestation of this escalation occurred in the US in 2001, when on Sunday, June 10, *The New York Times* sent discouraging shock waves across the country in a front-page article by David Barboza announcing that "experts" see an "inexorable" spread of genetically engineered crops, making it "almost impossible" for consumers to avoid them.[4]

Reactions of environmentally sensitive activists to the article are indications that it struck a nerve. As one committed environmentalist wrote: "This is just so painful to read. I feel as if a part of my being, my soul and body, has been yanked out of me, has been stolen and taken over by these companies."[5] To which another activist responded: "The reason you feel this way is because it is true. After all, the idea that our souls/bodies are separate from the souls/bodies of the living world around us is an illusion."[6]

Barboza's article itself is a mixture of truth and deceptive manipulation. It is problematic that the truth about the spread of contamination has struck sensitive readers and caused great pain. By conveying a picture of total hopelessness the author discouraged the will to fight back, to express opposition to genetic engineering. Presumably in order to present a balanced account, the author cites a statement by longtime critic of biotechnology Jeremy Rifkin, who is quoted as saying: "They're hoping there's enough contamination so that it's a fait accompli. But the liability will kill them. We're going to see lawsuits across the Farm Belt as conventional farmers and organic farmers find their product is contaminated."[7] However, Rifkin's seemingly hopeful statement is sandwiched between disheartening comments by biotech (i.e., nectech) supporters.

Barboza's piece is a blend of information and disinformation. Yet the experience itself of reading such an article and attending to our reactions can on some level be encouraging, because it reveals the depth of our felt connection with the living world. In such painful moments of revelation of our connectedness we sense that we have a choice.

The article invites us not only to recognize the extent of the contamination caused by genetic engineering but also to give up resisting. Barboza ends with a triumphal dismissal of "zero tolerance," citing Jeanne Romero-Severson, a professor of agriculture at Purdue University, who concludes: "If your standard is 100 percent pure, you better stop eating now."[8]

Trivial Resisters will not stop eating and we should not stop fighting. The Final Cause draws us onward, and it causes by attraction. When I speak of the Final Cause I mean:

> the indwelling, always unfolding goal or purpose, perceived as Good and attracting one to Act, to Realize her own participation in Be-ing; the beginning, not the end of becoming; the First Cause and Cause of causes, which gives an agent the motivation to Act; Radical Feminism, the Cause of causes.[9]

In ontological/thealogical[10] language, the ultimate Final Cause is She Who Attracts. She is Ultimate/Intimate Reality, the constantly Unfolding Verb of Verbs who is intransitive, who has no object that limits her dynamism. She is the Good who is Self-communicating, who is the Verb from whom, in whom, and with whom all true movements move. That is, She is, of course, Be-ing.

Goddess the Verb is hidden, for two reasons: First, there is our condition of living in the foreground, the deadly state of reversal. In this state our eyes have been dimmed and all of our senses numbed by *reversal*, which is defined in the *Wickedary* as

> [the] fundamental mechanism employed in the world-construction and world-maintenance of patriarchy; basic method employed in the making of patriarchal myths, ideologies, institutions, policies, and strategies; mad, master-minded maneuver characteristic of mirrordom: INVERSION—turning everything inside out and upside down. *Examples* a: the absurd story of Eve's birth from Adam b: the belief that man is superior to animals c: the worship of male divinity d: the belief that the Radical Feminist world view is "narrow" and/or "dated."[11]

The second reason why the Goddess is hidden is the inherent nature of the Final Cause, Who is, but is not yet—Who is always unfolding. There is an Element of Surprise. We participate in Her Creation—Knowing, yet UnKnowing, what we do.

The Final Cause is an invitation and a challenge to keep on Weaving and Moving. Defying gravity, we fly in the face of the spreading evil. Moving on, we find new Sisters/Resisters. We Discover and Realize deeper and wider connections in the Universe and Spin in Other Directions.

But this process is not simple. At times the connections, the Sisterhood especially, are not visible, tangible.

SPANNING THE GAPS

Sometimes Websters/Weavers/Spinsters lose our Way/ourSelves in the process of trying to Weave our way Out of the reversal world that is patriarchy. We become lost, weaving around, spinning our wheels, floundering in a world of bad imitations.

Through this experience—involving many events and much sorting out of temporarily lost memories and insights—often by reversing reversals—we Find ourSelves in an Other and Wilder World, which is the World of the Archaic Future. We become Luckier, better connected, so to speak, and more aware of *Syn-Crone-icities.*[12] Entering this New Time/Space, Be-Witching Hags/Harpies Happen upon Lost and Found Continent.

The expression "Lost and Found" implies that some loss/ losses precede the Finding. Women under patriarchy have always suffered losses, of course, and Wicked Women have always been finding and re-finding hidden treasures. It appears, however, that the early twenty-first century is a time of heightened experiences of Losing and Finding.

An Alarming Example of the Heightened Experience of Losing and Finding

In my book *Outercourse: The Be-Dazzling Voyage* I discussed my experiences of the publication of *Gyn/Ecology* (1979):

> I [wrote and] have always seen *Gyn/Ecology* as part of a Movement, including my own Voyage, which has continued since that writing and continues, because I am not a noun but a verb. When I set it free so it could *be* in the world, I did not see it as a work of perfection. For some women it could be an Awakening shock, for others a Source of information, or a springboard from which they might Leap into their own A-mazing Searches, Words, Metaphors.
>
> Above all, I was acutely aware that I had not done or written everything. I had not written the Last Word. (Otherwise, how could I ever write again?) Rather, I had set free this book, this Thunderbird, in the hope that its Call would be Heard. I hoped that it would soar together with the works of Other women, which were coming and would come from different Realms of the Background. I looked forward to the profusion of New Creation, which

I believed could emerge from women of all races, cultures, classes—from all over this planet—speaking/Be-Speaking out of our various and vital heritages.

From my Fourth Galactic perspective I see that this has happened and is happening, because our Time has come. Particularly Moving to me, personally, is the work of women of Ireland, that Treasure Island which I recognize deeply as the wellspring of my Background, my ancestral home. Especially Gynergizing on a global scale is the New abundance of creation from women of color.

Explosions of Diversity do not happen without conflict, however. One of the responses to *Gyn/Ecology* was a personal letter from Audre Lorde, which was sent to me in May 1979. For deep and complex personal reasons I was unable to respond to this lengthy letter immediately. However, when Lorde came to Boston to give a poetry reading that summer, I made a special effort to attend it, and spoke with her briefly. I told her that I would like to discuss her letter in person so that we would have an adequate opportunity to understand each other in dialogue, and I suggested places where we might meet for such a discussion. Our meeting did in fact take place at the Simone de Beauvoir Conference in New York on September 29, 1979. In the course of that hour-or-so-long meeting we discussed my book and her response. I explained my positions clearly, or so I thought. I pointed out, for example, in answer to Audre Lorde's objection that I failed to name Black Goddesses, that *Gyn/Ecology* is not a compendium of goddesses. Rather, it focuses primarily on those goddess myths and symbols which were direct sources of christian myth. Apparently Lorde was not satisfied, although she did not indicate this at the time. She later published and republished slightly altered versions of her originally personal letter to me in anthologies as an "Open Letter."

It continues to be my judgment that public response in kind would not be a fruitful direction. In my view, *Gyn/Ecology* is itself an "Open Book." . . . The writing of *Gyn/Ecology* was for me an act of Biophilic Bonding with women of all races and classes, under all the varying oppressions of patriarchy. Clearly, women who have a sincere interest in understanding and discussing this book have an obligation to read not only the statements of critics but also the book itself, and to *think* about it. . . .

LETTERS: THE SURGE OF BIOPHILIC BONDING

Throughout the horrors of the academented witchcraze the letters responding to *Gyn/Ecology* came to me. They came to me like healing balm. Reading many of them was and continues to be like sampling an almost infinite variety of exquisite wines. They renewed/Re-New my Spirit.

The letters conveyed many complex things. Simply stated, they poured out love and gratitude and they told me that the long struggle had not been in vain. They gave me something back—renewed Hope, Courage, and Strength. They surged up from the Subliminal Sea, with messages of Biophilic Bonding.[13]

Profoundly differing in tone and intent from these letters is Audre Lorde's piece ("Open Letter") which, as I wrote in *Outercourse*, has continued to be assigned

> as required reading by not a few professors in academentia to students in classes where *Gyn/Ecology* itself has not been assigned, or a mere handful of pages of this book have been required reading. This kind of selectivity is irresponsible. It imposes a condition of self-righteous ignorance upon students, often within the setting of "Women's Studies." This is, in my view, a worst case scenario of pseudoscholarship. It is, even if "well-intentioned," divisive, destructive. It functions, at least subliminally, as a self-protective statement about the purity and political correctness of the professor. It can be analyzed in further detail as a manifestation of the seven-point Sado-Ritual Syndrome, as described in *Gyn/Ecology* (pp. 130–33).[14]

My Lost and Found Letter to Audre Lorde

On September 22, 1979, I wrote to Audre Lorde responding to her letter of May 6, 1979, to me. She denied ever receiving this, insisting throughout the years, as she altered and republished her original letter to me, that I had never responded to her initial correspondence. Nearly a quarter of a century later, my "lost letter to Audre Lorde," with my last name written in Lorde's handwriting in the left bottom corner, was found amid her personal papers posthumously by her biographer, Alexis De Veaux, and documented in De Veaux's *Warrior Poet: A Biography of Audre Lorde*.[15]

The text of my letter is as follows:

September 22, 1979
Dear Audre,

First I want to thank you for sending me *The Black Unicorn*. I have read all of the poems, some of them several times. Many of them moved me very deeply—others seemed farther from my own experience. You have helped me to be aware of different dimensions of existence, and I thank you for this.

My long delay in responding to your letter by no means indicates that I have not been thinking about it—quite the contrary. I did think that by putting it aside for awhile I would get a better perspective than at first reaction. I wrote you a note to that effect which didn't get mailed since I didn't have your address. Then there was a hope of trying to get to Vermont in August, but the summer was overwhelmingly eventful.

Clearly there is no simple response possible to the matters you raise in your letter. I wrote *Gyn/Ecology* out of the insights and materials most accessible to me at the time. When I dealt with myth I used commonly available sources to find what were the controlling symbols behind judeo-christian myth in order to trace a direct line to the myths which legitimate the technological horror show. But of course to point out this restriction in the first passage is not really to answer your letter. You have made your point very strongly and you most definitely do have a point. I could speculate on how *Gyn/Ecology* would have been affected had we corresponded about this before the manuscript went to press, but it doesn't seem creativity-conducing to look backward. There is only *now* and the hope of breaking the barriers between us—of constantly expanding the vision.

I wonder if you will have any time available when I come to New York for the Simone de Beauvoir conference? Since I have a lot to do here, I had thought of just flying down Friday morning and returning that night. Are you free Friday afternoon or evening? Or will you be in Boston any time soon? I called and left a message on your machine. My number is.... Hope to see you and talk with you soon.

[Handwritten:] I hope you are feeling well, Audre. May the
strength of all the Goddesses be with you—Mary

I wrote this letter with the intention of communicating from
one Feminist to another, without thinking about publishing it or
preserving it for archives. So I did not focus on making a copy or
saving it to prove its existence. In 1979, I saw no need to make a
carbon copy or go out to a copy shop before mailing my letter to
Audre Lorde.

Imagine my surprise nearly a quarter of a century later, when,
on June 9, 2003, I was contacted by Alexis De Veaux, who was
asking my permission to quote from my unacknowledged and apparently "lost" letter of September 22, 1979. It was astonishing
after all these years to see someone—in fact, Audre Lorde's own
biographer—say that she had seen my letter among Lorde's personal papers. It was gratifying to read that De Veaux felt it was essential to publish my letter to Lorde in order to do justice to the
historical record—especially in light of the widespread public ac-
cusations and attacks resulting from Lorde's "Open Letter." De
Veaux was also determined to correct the prevailing belief that I
had not answered Lorde's letter and to honor the truth of my
reply.[16]

REALIZING OUR CONNECTEDNESS
AND POWERS OF CREATION

Some Trivial Women, shocked by the intensity of Lost and Found
experiences, proclaim that this must be the Time of Times for
manifestations of Trans-spatial/Transtemporal and Intergalactic
consciousness. We Sense that we are not alone in the universe. So
we are not hopelessly lost. If we are Desperate and Daring we can
continue to follow the Call of the Wild.

Such proclamations are most likely followed in the minds of
many readers by thoughts introduced by the word "But. . . ."

There are innumerable obstacles that women contemplate when preparing to make the Quantum Leaps required to bond in Sisterhood, save Life on earth, and have fun as well. The many blocks, mostly arising from the state of oppression, include depression, anxiety, loneliness, sickness, isolation, exhaustion, poverty, and the psychic/spiritual sabotage that accompanies and is engendered by all of these conditions. The blocks are expressed in "Buts," e.g., "But I am depressed, lonely, tired, afraid" et cetera, ad nauseam. Such blocks, real and imagined, are the sources of the "Buts," which in turn engender more blocks. Readers are invited to add their own lists of blocks and "Buts," thereby clearing the air.

Silly Women focusing on our Final Cause increasingly Realize our connectedness in Be-ing. We do not feel alone because we can Sense the benevolent Presences nearby. We can Leap with confidence, relaxing in the knowledge that we participate in a web of relationships within a unified whole.

This shift in emphasis from the parts to the whole has been exhibited in quantum physics since the 1920s. In the words of Werner Heisenberg, one of the originators of quantum physics, the world "appears as a complicated tissue of events, in which connections of different kinds alternate or overlap or combine and thereby determine the texture of the whole."[17] Fritjof Capra makes the point that quantum theory never ends up with "things." It always deals with interconnections.[18]

This conceptual shift from the parts to the whole pervaded other fields in the twentieth century as well. In the first half of that century the ideas of organismic biologists helped to give rise to "systems thinking." Capra explains:

> According to this view, the essential properties of an organism, or living system, are properties of the whole, which none of the parts have. They arise from the interactions and relationships among the parts.[19]

In recent decades biologists have been forced to acknowledge the importance of cooperation in the evolutionary process. This represents a radical shift of perception away from conventional evolutionary theory, specifically that of nineteenth-century Darwinists, who saw only competition in nature. Biologist Lynn Margulis shows that in contrast to conventional theorists who saw the unfolding of life as a process in which species continually diverge from one another, some modern biologists and ecologists are beginning to see continual cooperation and mutual dependence among all life forms as essential to evolution. As Lynn Margulis and Dorion Sagan state their refreshing view: "Life did not take over the globe by combat, but by networking."[20]

Drawing upon the work of Margulis and environmentalist James Lovelock, Fritjof Capra shows that in their "Gaia" theory these thinkers have explored the planetary dimensions of the unfolding of life. Capra points out that "our focus is shifting from evolution to coevolution—an ongoing dance that proceeds through a subtle interplay of competition and cooperation, creation and mutual adaptation."[21]

So Whatever Happened to the Final Cause?

Capra continues to soar in his analysis of the evolutionary unfolding of life over billions of years. He explains:

> Driven by the creativity inherent in all living systems, expressed through three distinct avenues—mutations, the trading of genes, and symbioses—and honed by natural selection, the planet's living patina expanded and intensified in forms of ever-increasing diversity.[22]

Then something strange seems to happen in his thought process. After acknowledging his intellectual debt to Lynn Margulis and Dorion Sagan, he suddenly announces:

> There is no evidence of any plan, goal, or purpose in the global evolutionary process and thus no evidence for progress; yet there are recognizable patterns of development.[23]

What seems to be going on here is a reduction of final causality to "plan, goal, or purpose" and an easy dismissal of the whole package on the basis that there is a "lack of [empirical] evidence." The classical concept of final causality is not even deemed worthy of mention. This reduces the analysis to the level of modern philosophy and Newtonian physics, which completely ignore the pivotal role of the "Cause of causes."

Such reductionism also marks the twenty-first-century pseudo-debate between "Creationism" and "Evolution," making this seem to be an either/or situation. What proponents on both sides fail to recognize is that there is an utterly Other way of thinking about these problems.

There is no lack of evidence for Final Causality, but this cannot be understood on the reductionist level of empirical evidence. When I write a book, for example, I Sense a beckoning, a calling, to bring this work into be-ing. I am motivated deep in my soul to produce this work, which is an outpouring of my soul. This Calling/Beckoning is an invitation to Realize my participation in Being through the creation of this particular work which is in itself a Beckoning to others to Realize their Selves through their own creativity.

What kind of "evidence" is there for the calling of the Final Cause, which is the Realization of Creativity? The answer lies in the realm where philosophy and mysticism meet. I can know that this process is happening, and this gives me intimations of the Creativity of the Universe. It is my own experience of the Cause of causes that opens the way to my conscious participation in the Creation of the Universe, and consequently to my real communication with other beings. It opens the way to expansion of Joy.

This process of consciously participating in the Attractive Power of the Final Cause demands Lusty Leaps of Courage to Create. And this brings us Leaping around further to deeply Hearing and Naming Goddess the Verb. She is the Goddess of many Names. Perhaps Now especially we are called to Hear her Fiercest Name, which is *Nemesis*.

Chapter Four

Realizing the Courage to Hear, Name, and Create Nemesis

In *Beyond God the Father* (1973) I wrote about Courage:

> The emerging creativity in women is by no means a merely cere-bral process. In order to understand the implications of this process it is necessary to grasp the fundamental fact that women have had the power of *naming* stolen from us.[1]

Behind and before that atrocity, however, is an even more deeply hidden one: Women have had the power of *Hearing* stolen from us. To understand the extent of this theft, we will do well to Hear the words of theologian Nelle Morton as she describes her first experience of "depth hearing":

> It was in a small group of women who had come together to tell our own stories that I first received a totally new understanding of hearing and speaking. I remember well how one woman started, hesitating and awkward, trying to put the pieces of her life together.... She talked on and on. Her story took on fantas-tic coherence. When she reached a point of most excruciating pain no one moved. No one interrupted. Finally she finished.

After a silence, she looked from one woman to another. "You heard me. You heard me all the way.... I have a strange feeling you heard me before I started. You heard me to my own story."[2]

Nelle goes on to explain that this experience happened again and again in other such small groups of women. She continues:

This woman was saying [i.e., Naming], and I had experienced, a depth hearing that takes place before the speaking—a hearing that is far more than acute listening. A hearing engaged in by the whole body that evokes speech—a new speech—a new creation. The woman *had* been heard to her own speech.[3]

This Dis-covering by Nelle Morton and those other women decades ago was "one of those essential dimensions of the full human experience long programmed out of our culture and our religious tradition."[4]

The Time Now, after the events of 9/11/01 and subsequent horrors, is a crucial Time for women to manifest the spiritual power of Hearing each Other beyond and through the inane/insane shouting of the "world's leaders." We can then hope to reclaim our own power of *Naming*, by which I mean:

Original summoning of words for the Self, the world, and ultimate reality; liberation by Wicked Women of words from confinement in the sentences of the fathers; Truth-telling: the only adequate antidote for phallocracy's Biggest Lies; exorcism of patriarchal labels by invoking Other reality and by conjuring the Spirits of women and of all Wild natures; Re-calling the Race of Radiant Words.[5]

However, even the Wildest of Women may sometimes feel daunted when surrounded and inundated by the doublespeak of a bush, an ashcroft, a powell, a rumsfeld, a sharon, a bin laden. Words like *truth, love, justice, evil, good* are churned into ashes when they leap at us from the newspaper, TV, or radio. They are transformed into hideous clanging noises when they come rush-

ing forth. Bombarding our ears and our minds with their meaninglessness, they become assault weapons against our souls.

How then can we save our souls? How can we escape and sur-
mount this foreground hell of Biggest Lies? We can Leap over the
patriarchs' war/wall of words by Hearing through them, refusing
to be distracted by them from Realizing our Powers. As I pointed
out in *Beyond God the Father,* "The liberation of language is rooted
in the liberation of our Selves."[6]

By Re-Calling our Powers we can Re-Call the Race of Radiant
Words. These Call from the Background, and when we Hear
them, they flow back, run back, shimmering and singing—reveal-
ing the foreground noises for what they are.

This happens when Wild Women practice Ontological
Courage in its various manifestations, including the Courage to
Hear Forth a New Semantic Field—a context in which the bul-
lies' Biggest Lies are cracked open—and Everything Changes....

Hmmm. I hear a very polite tapping at my door. It can't be my
rowdy friends from the Archaic Future. Could it be a neighbor?
No, it's not that kind of "normal" tapping. Well, maybe it's a ghost
from the past.

As I muttered this thought to Cottie, my Feline Familiar, I
heard a polite but loud and firm voice from the other side of the
door insisting: "I am *not* a ghost. I am *really* tired and thirsty and
I'm *very angry. Please open the door!*"

I jumped up and pushed the door open. The personage standing there was wearing a long dress and looked rather bedraggled,
but I recognized her immediately from her pictures, some of
which were affixed to my wall. "Matilda Joslyn Gage! How great
it is to see you!" I exclaimed. "Please come in!"

As I fell all over myself in my confused efforts at hospitality, the
determined Crone strode through the door and headed directly
for the poster on my wall which contained just one word: *Nemesis!* "Yes, that's a very important word!" she exclaimed. "That's
what I had in mind when I was writing my magnum opus,
Woman, Church and State." Anticipating the question I was about

to ask, she added: "No, I didn't use the word much, if at all, because, you know, I went as far as I could at that time. But you can see that the idea was there in my writings and speeches."

"I couldn't agree more," I said. "Listen to these words about you written by Sally Roesch Wagner in 1998:

> Her courage in almost single-handedly standing up to the oppressive forces of right-wing Christianity led to Gage being written out of official suffrage history."[7]

Gage acknowledged the passage with a serious nod. She strolled over to my desk and glanced at the 1998 anniversary edition of *Woman, Church and State,* politely refraining from touching it.

"Oh, please do pick it up, Matilda," I implored. "I would be so honored if you would read two of the great passages in Chapter X."

"Gladly," responded my guest, reaching eagerly for the beautiful volume.

"First, please read the first lines of the last paragraph on page 313," I requested.

Matilda read her own words with gusto:

> The most stupendous system of organized robbery known has been that of the church towards women. A robbery that has not only taken her self-respect but all rights of person, the fruits of her own industry, her opportunities of education, the exercise of her own judgment, her own conscience, her own will.[8]

She paused.

"Thank you, Matilda," I said with deep feeling. "Now, how about that great passage at the end of page 323? Would you be so generous as to read that?" I implored.

My guest was obviously very happy to oblige. Turning the pages eagerly, she pounced on the passage that she knew I wanted to hear and read her own words with enthusiasm:

Has woman no wrongs to avenge upon the church? As I look backward through history, I see the church everywhere stepping upon advancing civilization, hurling woman from the plane of "natural rights" where the fact of her humanity had placed her. And through itself and its control over the state, in the doctrine of "revealed rights," everywhere teaching an inferiority of sex, a created subordination of woman to man making her very existence a sin; holding her accountable to a diverse code of morals from man, declaring her possessed of fewer rights in church and in state—her very entrance into heaven made dependent upon some man to come as mediator between her and the Savior it has preached—thus crushing her personal, intellectual and spiritual freedom.[9]

"Hooray, Matilda," I shouted. "You Go, girl!"

And she did. She disappeared! "Oh, no, Matilda! I wasn't telling you to leave. That's just a contemporary expression of approval and encouragement!"

Somehow I Knew that she had gotten my message and that this was just a parting joke.

But she is really very Present Now. I've gotten Matilda's message. She is saying: "It's Time for women to become en-Gaged!"[10]

THE TRANSFORMATIVE POWERS
OF HEARING AND NAMING

In *Gyn/Ecology*, patriarchy was Named "the state of fear." In the *Wickedary* it was described succinctly as "state created, supported, and legitimated by ceaseless terrorism: phallocracy, snooldom."[11] In *Quintessence*, this concept is further developed:

As the patriarchal death marchers relentlessly strut into their "millennial time," they work to undermine the Expanding Presence of Elemental Women. Wild Women witness and experience ubiquitous terrorism, striving to thrive through and beyond the increasing horrors of the state of atrocity, in which abominations are normalized, ritualized, repeated, legitimized, sacralized.[12]

Toward the end of that chapter in *Quintessence* I found mySelf Leaping with the Joy of once again expelling the demonic/ necrophilic chokers of life. I was coming more into touch with native Biophilic Intelligence, Realizing the Elemental Genius that flows through and pervades all the Elements and which is the deep unifying principle accessible to Trivial Women:

> At the very core of Elemental Feminist Genius is power to transform the imposed state of isolation and fragmentation into Magnetic Expanding Presence. Each dispersed participator in such Genius can Magnetize Others, who, of course, are Magnetizing her.
> This is the Power most feared by phallocrats, whose aim is to destroy Elemental life. For this reason they perpetually lie. They try to erase, convert, maim, dismember, and assimilate all women and especially all who are bearers of Radical Elemental consciousness. When women Realize our own Genius, the necrophiliac sir nothings will shrivel into the nothingness which is their self-made identity.[13]

Magical, Magnetic Naming can happen in a communal way— in an ontologically, politically powerful way—only if women Hear ourSelves and each Other Deeply. Such Hearing can happen when we exercise the Courage to Hear through the deafening droning of the deadheads who are the dictators of dickocracy (e.g., the bushes, blairs, bin ladens, sharons, et cetera). We then block out the babble and blow away the bubbles of the babblespheres/ bubblespheres that constitute the phallocentric discourse of deadland/daddyland. When we Hear our way through all the twisted mazes of hot air we begin to exercise Truly Transformative Powers of Naming Background Reality.

By the Magnetism of our Hearing and Naming we summon and attract the Energy/Gynergy needed for Acts of Leaping with *Amazon Grace.*

LUSTY LEAPING IN THE TIME OF TIMES

Extreme Times present the conditions for Extreme Leaps. This chapter is being written in such an opportune Time. The Actual

Time is Now. September 11, 2001, has come and gone, leaving its stench all around, generating more of the same. The foreground temporal and spatial location is the state of fear: the state of stench, the state of stealth. Which is also

... the state of animated death

... the state of appeasement

... the state of atrocity

... the state of boredom/snoredom

... the state of captivity and contamination

... the state of clonedom, which clones itself into other/same states including confusion, deception, degradation, despair, diaspora, dividedness, isolation, living death, mass hypnosis, patriarchal paralysis, perpetual distraction, possession, predatory prickery, separation, severance, staledom, terror, torture, total tokenism, et cetera, ad nauseam.

Which is to say: This is the epitome of patriarchy, the peak of prickery, beyond and outside of which Lusty Leaping can really happen. Indeed, it appears that the only way Out Now is by taking such Leaps.

BE-LAUGHING INTO THE BACKGROUND

The deadly seriousness that prevails in the early twenty-first century is appalling to those women who can see this as a sign of spiritual decay. Strong, Hearty Hags have always known the power of Elemental Laughter to crack man-made pseudo-reality. Elemental Laughing is an expression of deep Knowing. It is a cognitive triumph over the prevailing paralysis of the higher faculties. It is an assertion of sanity in the hideous reversal world thrust upon us by idiotic governments and moronizing media. Elemental Laughter is extremely important as a signal of bonding and compatibility, and it generates both.

The Elemental Laughing of Wild Women (Background Laughing) is a major manifestation of intellectual strength and a declaration of independence from the prevailing mentality. It is totally Other from foreground laughter, which signals submission to the prevailing stereotypes, rules of acceptable behavior, and, in general, Self-censorship. Background Laughter also signals rejection of ideas, behavior, and realities that might be perceived as threatening. It is utterly unlike canned laughter/humor that is required by patriarchally controlled/patrolled rules of politeness— and it is an Amazonian antidote to canned seriousness, such as that typically manifested in and prescribed by sunday sermons, the nightly news, and academented assemblies and conferences.

It is this aspect of Be-Laughing (Big Laughing), i.e., actively/alarmingly expressed refusal to deny Deep Knowledge and Naming of threatening reality, which marks it as a major manifestation of the Weird Wisdom of Wild Women. We are developing our Powers of Hearing and Naming the attacks we now face from the killers who are running this planet—attempting to run us down.

The thrusting throng of thugs/patriarchs lunge and push ahead with their project—the penetration, mangling, and murder of the planet and all life; this entails shoving women and all ecosystems off balance. WE MUST ACQUIRE THE COURAGE TO SEE THIS AND TO LIVE AND ACT ACCORDINGLY. We must strive to get back our balance. We can and must regain our ability to Be and Act in our own Space, and on our own terms. This is the proprioception we need in order to Survive and Thrive. We must push aside the pushy pack of predators who would paralyze and prevent Life-Loving Lusty women, animals, winds, waters, stars, dandelions, and trees from the attainment of our Birthright—our full participation in creation—that is, our Right to Leap.

So what is it that is holding us back?

PARALYSIS BY THE MECHANISMS OF DEADLY DENIAL

It is worth our while to examine a phenomenon that is working to stop us dead, that is, deadly denial. Consider how this works together with reversal to kill awareness of the ecological crisis which is upon us. These mechanisms prevent our Deep Hearing and Naming the hideous reality of climate change, also known as "global warming."

Denial of the fact of climate change throughout the last decade of the twentieth century and continuing into the present century has involved denial of the atrocities involved—the drastic shifts in weather patterns, the floods and droughts, the alarming melting of ice in polar regions, the increasingly desperate migrations of animals and people, the devastating shortages and contamination of food and water.

Consider, moreover, the fact that denial of these realities involves deadening/deadending our capacity to See and Name and Feel Deeply the interconnections/innerconnections among these apparently disparate phenomena. Denial entrenches us in patterns of fragmented thinking and feeling. Consequently it amounts to a colossal impairment of our capacities for cognition and creative action. It undermines/kills Creative Hope.

As the disease of deadly denial expands exponentially to obscure these obvious manifestations of impending doom for all life on this planet, seemingly inexplicable feelings of meaninglessness, depression, foreboding, and terror are pushed down into unconsciousness. These unexpectedly erupt in the form of impotent gestures and frenzied activities, such as obsessive and greedy accumulation of money and things.

On a vast scale these unheard, unnamed, and suppressed feelings and recognitions of the pervasive horror explode in massive and escalating acts of violence, such as the inherently insane and ever-expanding "war on terrorism."

In this context we can glimpse an explanation for the popularity of the unelected "president" George W. Bush and his ever-escalating "war on terror." In June 2002 Eric Alterman, writing in *The Nation*, while attempting to explain G. W. Bush's 2000 "victory," observed that the media pulled this off by spending "millions upon millions covering the candidates while reporting next to nothing of value to voters."[14] He explained that the media focused on "personality" and associated asininity. The media disastrously misfocused, but blaming the media doesn't explain the dilemma, which Alterman described in one brief sentence: "By any conventional calculation, Bush should have lost in a landslide." Alterman fails to answer his own refreshingly forthright question: "Are people just stupid?"[15]

Consider the possibility that "people"—including the media moguls, the Supreme Court, the politicians, and the journalist himself—are just possessed and stultified by the State of Denial—Big Time.

How could a population that is blind to the obvious attempts to murder the planet and its inhabitants manage to See through the massive corruption of the society that generates media which blind them?

EXPLOSIONS OF CONSCIOUSNESS AND ACTION

Paralyzed by patriarchy, the State of Denial, which has reached a zenith of madness, how can we begin the process of undenying? Take one step at a time—any step.

Let's start with a simple statement of fact. The expression "war on terrorism" is nonsensical. War IS terrorism. The nonlogical babble is beyond and beneath the doublespeak of George Orwell's 1948 novel, *1984*.

But now there is another "George," also known as "shrub" and as "Bush the dumber," who apparently does not even grasp that he is mouthing fiction, which of course he has been programmed to memorize. This semi-literate graduate of one of America's "most illustrious universities," where he belonged to an influential club known as "Skull and Bones," is living proof of the cynicism of "higher education" and its administrators and products. So who cares if he spews empty words about "nucular" power? Who even notices?

And who minds if a pinhead is president? (There have been others.) After the farce of his first "election," it is clear that the title "President Bush" is an oxymoron anyway. Some people have noticed that. However, maybe minds are getting duller, very rapidly. Consider the 2003 election of movie star, action-figure Governor Arnold Schwarzenegger in California. Do we turn aside in deep disgust or just Laugh Out Loud? Does it matter?

Still there is the continued Reality of Realizing Hope. Hopeful Wild Women Realize Our Real Presence. This is our Presence to Our Selves and to each Other. It is Female Elemental participation in Powers of Be-ing. When we Realize this we are Weaving and Re-Weaving the fabric of unseen connectedness. Steadily—as well as by Leaps and Bounds—we can continue to build up morphogenetic fields, making possible Quantum Leaps over the walls of the prisons which are patriarchy's religions, professions, ideologies, sciences, technologies, politics, great art, nightly news, et cetera.

But in order to facilitate such Lusty Leaping, Trivial Women may need special Jolts.

Chapter Five

What Terrific Shock Will Be Shocking Enough?

THE EXTENT AND DEPTH OF DAMAGE inflicted by phallocracy on Self-consciousness is ineffable and unfathomable. To begin to See this, and then to Name it and Act consistently with this Seeing and Naming, women may require an experience of great shocks which can move us into a state of shock. Our Foresister Susan B. Anthony believed this. In 1870 she wrote:

> So while I do not pray for anybody or any party to commit out-rages, still I do pray, and that earnestly and constantly, for some terrific shock to startle the women of this nation into a self-respect which will compel them to see the abject degradation of their pres-ent position; which will force them to break their yoke of bondage, and give them faith in themselves, which will make them proclaim their allegiance to women first; which will enable them to see that man can no more feel, speak, or act for women than could the old slaveholder for his slave.[1]

In the first decade of this century Susan B. Anthony's prayer of 1870 might seem to have been partially answered. G. W. Bush and his sordidly submissive Environmental Protection Agency delivered a "terrific shock" to this nation by abandoning all attempts at denying that climate change is real, ongoing, and manmade, and then, without missing a beat, continuing to insist on NO CHANGE in US policy that would deal with this horrendous threat. Bush & company even suggested that we can "adapt" and rely upon "voluntary efforts" to reduce US emissions of carbon dioxide and other air pollutants.[2]

The "shock" of this ongoing travesty is experienced not only by some women, of course, but also by some men, many of whom have been outstanding opponents of environmental destruction. So how does this connect with Susan B. Anthony and her prayer for a shock that would startle women, specifically? To work our way toward an answer to this complex question, consider the implications of the fact that the successive heads of the EPA appointed by G. W. have conveniently functioned as token torturers of our Sister the Earth and her nonhuman and human inhabitants.

What feelings and thoughts does this simple fact elicit in a woman who identifies as a Feminist and who cares profoundly about the fate of the Earth and its inhabitants? There is a sense of disappointment and horror. But often this is blended with a bland, matter-of-fact, sophisticated acceptance of "reality": "Of course," says our bland feminist, "they're Bush appointees, so what can you expect?"

Over a quarter of a century ago I published in *Gyn/Ecology* an analysis of assimilation, psychic numbing, token torturers, and the state of total tokenism. It may be that in the expanding state of total tokenism in this century most women have become incapable of experiencing great shocks. Perhaps the worse the shocks women have had to endure, the greater our susceptibility to psychic numbing. In the early twenty-first century the media's portrayals of everyday atrocities against women and nature all over the globe have given heightened meaning to Hannah Arendt's expression "the banality of evil."

This observation leads to the thought that in the state of shock we are knocked into an unshockable state.

The self-contradiction and dilemma attached to the condition of "shock" would seem to put a damper on Susan's famous prayer for a "terrific shock." Was she praying for the wrong thing? Not exactly; I believe that her use of the word "shock" is an indication that she was on the trail of Something Big.

Although Susan could not then adequately articulate the Wondrous Positively Shocking Reality which can hurl us beyond the self-contradiction, she intuited its existence. Indeed, her heroic life is itself a manifestation of this Reality.

The dilemma arises from hearing and saying the word *shock* only from a foreground perspective. Shocks that are caused by the deadbeat daddies of daddyland are simply not Terrific enough. Since they are mere foreground phenomena, they inevitably keep us stuck in a maze of contradictions. The "outrages" of fatherland, no matter how hideous and destructive, cannot of themselves be the answer to Susan's prayer. They cannot Shock us Out of the phallocentric foreground and into the Magnificent and Infinitely Shocking Background. For this, something Other is needed.

The Shock of Be-ing

All Wild creatures and Other realities participate in Be-ing, by which I mean "Ultimate/Intimate Reality, the constantly Unfolding Verb of Verbs which is intransitive, having no object that limits its dynamism."[3] The Terrific Shock of encountering and Realizing Be-ing is utterly unlike the foreground shocks which keep us imprisoned and circling the masters' mazes. The Shock of meeting Be-ing is simple and direct. It is absolutely surprising and joyous. It is Self-transformative and changes Everything. It is unforgettable. It opens pathways that go on and on. It makes one Realize how Lucky she is. The Prayer that comes to mind is "Thank you! Thank you!"

Be-ing manifests in natural creatures. A clover blossom announces: "I am." The girl or woman sitting on the grass who just "happens" to Hear these words is astonished but not afraid. The simplicity and naturalness of the event—its ordinariness—does not conflict with its extraordinariness. It simply Is, and subtly everything changes.

This means that the woman who has met the ontologically articulate clover blossom (or pebble or blade of grass or tree or piece of ice in the snow) gradually is enabled also to meet the foreground shocks in a different way. Having encountered Background Reality that is everywhere in nature, Be-Speaking in the Chorus of Be-ing, she becomes more Adventurous. She is surrounded by Natural Friends, as she follows her own path. She is a creator. When it is necessary she confronts the evil foreground world, taking on the attackers and oppressors of women and nature with confidence and Daring.

She is aided always, all ways by Amazon Grace, which manifests as an ontological experience.

THE INTUITION OF BE-ING

In a footnote in *Beyond God the Father* I commented on Jacques Maritain's analysis of his "intuition of being":

> Although he was hardly a feminist or social revolutionary, Maritain had an exceedingly fine sensitivity to the power of this intuition, which, if it were carried through to social consciousness, would challenge the world.[4]

And, I now add, it could be an answer to Susan's Prayer. On the face of it, linking Jacques Maritain and Susan B. Anthony might seem a bit odd. The result of this linkage might appear to be an Odd Couple. So? We live in an odd world.

The origin of this "marriage" is my own experience and intellectual history as a Radical Feminist philosopher. My own existential encounter with a clover blossom happened when I was about fourteen years old. I was lying on the grass after a dip in a local swimming hole in Schenectady, New York. Suddenly the clover blossom spoke two words. It said: "I am." I recall being shocked and amazed, but the experience was not heavy. Rather it was apparently casual and it was gentle. I had the impression that the clover blossom was making a statement about itSelf—not trying to show off or overwhelm me but simply making a point. Despite the astonishing speech it had made, which would change my life, it appeared to be, well, just blossoming.

I couldn't ever forget this experience. I'm not sure whether I told anyone about it at that time. I had never heard of an intuition like this and had no words for this event. But my life was suffused with it. It guided me on paths I was supposed to follow. I know that it was connected with my ever-growing conviction that I wanted to become a philosopher, even though I couldn't know exactly what that word meant. Certainly it would never have occurred to anyone in those times at Saint Joseph's Academy, the parochial high school I attended during the 1940s in Schenectady, New York, to speak to a teenage girl about the call to become a philosopher. But it didn't matter. The clover blossom had taken care of all that.

Then there was my brief but everlasting affair with a hedge on the campus of Saint Mary's College, at Notre Dame, Indiana. I was about twenty-three and was studying for my doctorate at the School of Sacred Theology, which had been established by the poet Sister Madeleva Wolfe, then president of Saint Mary's, who wanted to do something about the fact that women were not allowed to study catholic theology for a Ph.D. anywhere in the US.

One morning I happened to walk past a hedge on my way to class. It spoke two words to me. These words were: "Continued existence." I realized eventually that this was a companion intuition to the earlier one, making explicit the duration of the verb "I am," which refers to participation in Be-ing. It Announced a Now that always Is.

By the time I encountered Maritain's work in the early sixties (while studying for my doctorate in philosophy in Fribourg, Switzerland), I was ready for his books on the "intuition of being." His work was useful and inspiring. However, with the surging of the Women's Revolution in the late sixties, and especially in the seventies, eighties, nineties, and—yes—in the twenty-first century, it has become ever more obvious to me that the ontological intuition is about Be-ing the Verb and that it must be "carried through to social consciousness, which will challenge the world."[5]

The word *being*, of course, can function both as a verb and as a noun. When people speak of "the Supreme Being" this refers to a noun. One cannot participate in this. It just hangs "up there." My use of the hyphen in Be-ing is intended to indicate that I am referring exclusively to the Verb, which is Ultimate/Intimate Reality in which we (all creatures) participate by be-ing ourSelves.

The Terrific Shock that Susan B. Anthony was praying for could not come from encountering the "supreme being" (supreme block). Blocks cannot Shock. Be-ing, on the Other hand, Unblocks/Shocks. It opens the way for infinite possibilities.

Bearing this in mind, we revisit Susan's pertinent words (cited earlier) for further revelations.

In her remarkable passage Susan describes the reasons for praying for the shock. First, she wanted it "to startle the women of this nation into a self-respect which will compel them to see the abject degradation of their present position." The first consequence of the "terrific shock," then, is that women are startled into self-respect. This would not be an immediate effect of a foreground shock (for example, being molested). Indeed, when we consider the array of feelings associated with such an atrocious event—shame, fear, anger, disappointment, horror—it is unlikely that Self-respect would leap out, since this is precisely what is under attack.

However, if we think about the reaction of a woman who experiences the gift of an Intuition of Be-ing, Susan's choice of words clearly fits very accurately. The recipient of this revelation has experienced Depth Hearing (Nelle Morton's expression). She senses that she is Lucky and is honored to have received this grace, and is therefore startled into Self-respect.

Moreover, Susan is completely accurate in her observation that it is such Self-respect that will compel women to see the abject degradation of their present position and give them faith in themselves.

The Self-respect which is elicited when a woman experiences an Intuition of Be-ing naturally compels her to see the grotesque inappropriateness of her degraded position and that of all women. The contrast is glaringly obvious, intolerable, and wrong—so wrong that it forces her to break her insufferable "yoke of bondage." She is driven to break out, and she is enabled to do this because she has begun to Dis-cover Faith in herSelf. Moreover, her Acts of Seeing and Breaking Out of bondage and gaining faith in herself constitute a continuing Spiraling process, with each Act leading to another. This is the way the dynamism of the Intuition of Be-ing works to recharge the Spiraling of consciousness and action.

Moreover, this Spiraling movement works communally as well as individually. Anthony, a Feminist Activist, wrote this passage in the plural. The use of the plural is particularly interesting to note as a theme: Communal movement is not merely collective. Rather it is interactive. As participants in Be-ing women act upon each Other. The actions of each participant not only spur her on to further Acts: e.g., of Seeing, Breaking Out, and Gaining Faith in her-Self. But also, by these further Acts each woman Gynergizes each other woman. These interactive movements constitute a complex Cosmic Dance of Be-ing. They are participation in the Creative work of the Goddess (or, as some would say, "Goddessing").

The next Leap in Susan's analysis of the effects upon women of the "terrific shock" is that (because it will give them faith in themselves) it "will make them proclaim their allegiance to women first." This is the dramatic Leap to the Core of Radical Elemental Feminism. It is the taboo-breaking, threatening Leap, at the

mention of which the fainthearted tremble and turn back. It is at
this point that Susan reveals her true identity as Wild Woman,
Positively Revolting Hag, Powerful Crone. In the Light and
Wind of these words we See/Hear that she is no mere "equal
rights feminist." She is actively participating in the powers and
work of the Goddess Nemesis, Elementally disrupting the patriarchal balance of terror, Passionately Spinning/Spiraling Archaic
Threads of *Gynergy*.

Susan is uncompromising: Women who proclaim their allegiance to women first See that "man can no more feel, speak, or
act for woman than could the old slaveholder for his slave." Her
speech crescendos:

> The fact is, women are in chains, and their servitude is all the more
> debasing because they do not realize it. O, to compel them to see
> and feel, and to give them the courage and conscience to speak and
> act for their own freedom, though they face the scorn and con-
> tempt of all the world for doing it![6]

It is Time Now for our Deep Hearing of this Great Hag's De-
fiant Howl!

The Morphic Resonance of the Prayers and Other Acts of Great Foresisters

Great Foresisters are Be-Speaking to us Now. They are Auguring,
Foretelling, Speaking of what will be. They are bringing about
psychic/material change by means of words. They are Be-Speaking us further and further into Be-ing.

They are Naming our interconnectedness, which involves
Transtemporal/Trans-spatial Consciousness, Communication,
Sisterhood, Conversations, Synchronicities, Syn-Crone-icities,
Telepathic Travels.

Women who are Trivial enough to Sense and Act upon the
messages of our Foresisters can confront the nothingness of the

nothing-loving technomaniacs and Realize our Hope in our Selves. We do not feel unfamiliar with the interconnectedness of the quantum universe. Nor are we alienated by the thought that, instead of being empty, space is filled with unseen connections. Indeed, this is our common experience, and it makes possible Faith in the worth of our particular works and acts, which have wide-ranging effects.

While Re-Calling the words and works of our famous Fore-sisters, we also Sense and acknowledge the achievements of those whose names and creations have been stolen and erased in patri-archal history (even as our own names and creations are being stolen and erased in fatherland today). The influence of our For-gotten Foresisters is felt by Wild Women, who note that in as-trology *influence* means "an emanation of occult power held to derive from stars" (*Webster's*). These Foresisters are indeed like Stars whose Light and Spiritual Force flow to us/through us, pro-ducing Gynergy. They are our Hidden Power Sources, hurling Secret Weapons to Amazons, pouring into us our true Archaic Heritage, which is the Abundance of Amazon Grace.

As Wild Women actively receive this Heritage we become transmitters as well as creators. We participate in Foresisterhood, passing on the torches of our own tradition. We actualize the an-swer to Susan's prayer and to the prayers of all the Foresisters by Seeing, Feeling, Couraging, Speaking, and Acting for our own freedom. By Be-Speaking beyond the scorn and contempt of the fathers' world, we become the answer.

We also become like Stars, emanating Occult Power, influenc-ing our Sisters. So it is that Trivial Women's experiences of unseen connectedness also inspire Fantastic Daring and increasing Self-confidence. As Travelers and Weavers in a participative universe we increasingly trust our own judgment even when our reasons are not evident to others.

This progress happens especially when we learn to Sense the presence of morphogenetic fields. Weird Searchers proclaim that through the influence of Prayers and Dreams of all our

Foresisters the evolution of Feminist consciousness continues, and these influences do not fall off with distance in space or time. They are Here Now.

SO WHAT IS DIFFERENT ABOUT
THE EARLY TWENTY-FIRST CENTURY?

The sense of all-pervasive nightmare-ishness did not come all at once. The creepy sense that "something is out of joint" had been present for years/decades/centuries, but it had somehow been possible to tune out the horror, at least enough to relax at times.

By the first decade of the twenty-first century, for some of us at least, the collusion/collision of seemingly disparate horrors had become increasingly obvious. Looking at the first page of *The New York Times* (or any first page of almost any newspaper) can be a way of getting the big picture "in your face."

The effect of this barrage of bad news is overwhelming. Typically our reader seeks escape, feeling a sense of helplessness and meaninglessness, perhaps to the point of nausea. Her Rage is somehow blocked, because of an apparent inability to know what connections exist among these disastrous events. Who or what is the source of them? Specifically, no one—certainly not the newspaper—Names the overriding cause of such evils.

Something is missing. It appears that "no one" is able to find a connecting thread among these horrors. Yet thirty years ago (and twenty years ago, and ten years ago, and even ten minutes ago) *many women* have seen the blatant thread. We have Named it in our multiple and powerful expressions of Gynergy—our books, our classes, our workshops, our speeches, our conversations, our political activism, our mutual support and loyalty to each other. We Named/Name it with the Wicked Old Word *patriarchy*. For the sake of clarity and convenience to the readers of this book, I will Here and Now Howl Out again the meaning of this word, which I have elaborated upon in *Beyond God the Fa-*

ther, in all of my books, and definitively defined in the *Wickedary* as follows:

> 1: society manufactured and controlled by males: FATHERLAND; society in which every legitimated institution is entirely in the hands of males and a few selected henchwomen; society characterized by oppression, repression, depression, narcissism, cruelty, racism, classism, ageism, [speciesism,] objectification, sadomasochism, necrophilia; joyless society, ruled by Godfather, Son, and Company; society fixated on proliferation, propagation, procreation, and bent on the destruction of all Life 2: the prevailing religion of the entire planet, whose essential message is necrophilia.[7]

Patriarchy, discredited as passé and associated with the "jargon" of dated "seventies feminism" and the rhetoric of loathsome *Radical Feminism,* is often looked upon in academic circles as less than unworthy of notice. It is too embarrassingly obvious to deserve mention by erudite professors and sophisticated graduate students of feminist theory. That foolish term *patriarchy* MUST BE KEPT BURIED, they assume, together with bustles and bloomers, in the attics of women's history.

So what sort of Revolting Hag would dig up this threadbare term and haul it out for display in this decade of this century? I, MARY DALY, AM THE SORT OF EMBARRASSING AND POSITIVELY REVOLTING HAG WHO WOULD DO SUCH AN INAPPROPRIATE ARCHEOLOGICAL DIG, AND I AM DOING IT HERE, NOW!

So the question then arises: Who or what caused (and continues to cause) the discrediting and erasure of a word, such as *patriarchy,* that so aptly Names the enemy of women and all of the oppressed, including our planet herSelf? Whose interest is served by this discrediting of language that enables women to Be-Speak important connections and subsequently to think and articulate coherent and liberating thoughts? Could it be that such word-suffocation benefits those who also discredit expressions like *Radical Feminism?* And could it be that such word-obliteration serves the purposes of those who wish to discredit and disappear our Fore-sisters themselves, thus destroying the possibility of Wild Women connecting with each Other and ourSelves? AND WE DO KNOW THAT FURIOUS FEMALE BONDING COULD OBLITERATE PATRIARCHY ITSELF, DON'T WE?

SO LET'S DO IT!

I leave it to the Courageous reader to answer these questions, trusting that the morphic resonance of our Foresisters of the Past will carry her through the maze of lies, distortions, and silences of the foreground now and into a truly Archaic Present and Future.

CHAPTER SIX

QUANTUM LEAPING AHEAD/BACK TO LOST AND FOUND CONTINENT

2056 BE (BIOPHILIC ERA)

TO SILLY WOMEN WITH SOME EXPERIENCE of Intergalactic Travel and Communication it will not seem implausible that my Naming of Foresisters of the Past can reignite connections with Foresisters of the Future. To those who first read *Quintessence* when it appeared in 2048 BE (Biophilic Era) or in subsequent years of this Era it will seem quite natural that this Naming can be a kind of Conjuring of the inhabitants of Lost and Found Continent in 2056 BE. The morphogenetic resonance of these Future Feminists is in harmony with the Archaic Past, and the resonance is cumulative.

It is Stunning to contemplate the Power of such Influence/ Confluence. Realizing this Power gives Hope and the possibility of Really recognizing the shriveled up nothingness of patri- archy/snooldom and its minions. If Wild Women today Sense this Foresisterly/For-Sisterly Power, which Whirls and Spirals from Archaic Past to Archaic Future and back and around again and again, we can be buoyed up by its Spiraling Presence and become truly Present ourSelves in the process of creation.

There is great danger, however, that we will fail to Seize the Moment—right Now! Some women in the early twenty-first century—among them many idealistic feminists—have become discouraged by the vituperative foreground lies and the hardships heaped upon us and have almost stopped believing in our own Cause.

So do we want to settle for becoming self-pitying, dulled-out dummies, when the Archaic Future is SO CLOSE THAT WE CAN TOUCH IT, which is to Say, RIGHT HERE? To fail at this Time, by choosing to lack Courage, Generosity, Faith, and Hope is to choose the triumph of evil.

Recently I heard mySelf Howling these words. They were not coming just from me, but also from the Winds (think hurricanes), the Waters (think floods, think melted permafrost in Alaska), the Fires (think forest fires across the US and throughout the rain forests, think drought), and the Earth, our Mother and Sister, who continues to endure the man-made atrocities against herSelf and her innocent offspring—the soil, the trees, the animals, the children (think nuclear holocaust, think global warming).

Feeling a shift in the morphogenetic field, I continued to Howl loudly: "I DON'T CARE WHO IS LISTENING!"

About to shout even louder, I was stopped dead in my Howling by yet another shift in the field, followed by the sound of a familiar pleasant voice.

"You don't have to yell! We're not hard of hearing, and we're wide awake Here on Lost and Found Continent! And of course you do care who is Listening. That's why I came to speak with you. You Invoked me!"

Looking up from my computer screen, I saw someone ambling down the path right outside my window. "Annie!" I exclaimed in a spasm of surprise and joy. "How did you get there?"

By the time I could jump up from my desk and rush outside I realized that "there" is actually right Here. In other words, I was transported to Lost and Found Continent. To be specific, we were running to greet each other on the path in Annie's garden in 2056 BE. The shock was almost overwhelming.

After we hugged and danced around with some of the many animals who were playing in the garden, we sat down on the stone bench under an apple tree and began to speak simultaneously.

"Whoa!" said Annie. "We're both talking at the same time. I can't even hear mySelf."

A squirrel hopped up between us and started chattering. "Look!" I said. "She seems to be making fun of us. OK, you go first, Annie. It seems so long since your 'Anonyma Network' brought out the 2048 BE Edition of *Quintessence!* I need to get my bearings, before I can talk coherently. It's been a rough time back 'there/then' at the end of the 1990s a.d. and the beginning of the twenty-first century!" Sensing that I was drifting off to sleep, I slid off the bench onto the grass, while managing to explain, "I'm exhausted! Hope you don't mind if I lie on the grass here for a while."

When I woke up, refreshed by my nap, I found that both Annie and the squirrel had joined me on the grass. Annie had spread a cloth on the ground, on which she was assembling an inviting lunch, consisting of nuts and berries for the squirrel (who didn't wait for the party to begin formally and began munching right away), together with sandwiches, cakes, apples, and peaches for the rest of us. I then spotted Annie's mother, Kate, hurrying down from her house with a jug of "Lost and Found" lemonade and cups for the three of us.

"Oh, hello, Kate!" I cried out, jumping up to greet her. "It's so wonderful to see you again!" We all stood there, beaming at each other blissfully.

It took Kate's solid sense of realism to bring us back to earth, so to speak. "For Juno's sake! Let's sit down and enjoy the feast!" she commanded. Without another word, we all plunged in.

While we lunged for the sandwiches Kate asked wryly, "Well, Mary, how were things going for you, back there/then before your Present trip to Lost and Found?"

I choked on my sandwich so loudly that Annie had to pound me on the back. I finally responded. "You know how things were going, generally speaking, Kate, because you were there/then—at least until just before you and the Other Members of Anonyma Network took off for Lost and Found Continent. Of course, we never crossed paths then, but you know from your own experience what it was like already in the late twentieth century. To mention a few 'details': There was environmental devastation, including land degradation caused by intensive agribusiness and other human activities. And there was massive deforestation which, together with a huge rise in carbon dioxide emissions, contributed to atmospheric build-up of carbon and resulted in global warming, also known as Climate Change. This was manifested in phenomena such as floods, droughts, windstorms, raging forest fires. And it just kept getting worse."

A number of animals and women who had been quietly eavesdropping were now visibly and audibly moving closer. The attentiveness of this growing audience spurred me on. Feeling shaken by everything I had just disclosed, I was unable to stop my rapid recitation of environmental horrors.

So I went on: "In addition to all of this was the problem of nuclear waste and radiation. According to the International Atomic Agency the total global stockpile of spent nuclear fuel in 2000 was 220,000 tons, and it was growing by approximately 10,000 tons each year. Chemical pollution spread virtually everywhere. By the year 2000 pesticides had become between ten and one hundred times more toxic than in the mid-1970s. And it kept on spreading."

Since my audience was stunned into silence, I continued. "Huge epidemics spread, particularly in Africa. Deaths from HIV/AIDS increased more than sixfold worldwide between 1990 and 2000. Most of these deaths occurred in sub-Saharan Africa. Millions died in Africa from tuberculosis and malaria."

Desperately propelled onward by the frozen silence around me, I said, "The problem of fresh water scarcity was the most overwhelming nightmare. In 2002 water shortages killed over seven million people. Six thousand children died every day from drinking polluted water."

Noticing that I was becoming exhausted and parched by my grim recitation, Kate poured more lemonade. I accepted this gratefully and continued. "In fact, the UN reported that in 2002 about 1.2 billion people worldwide were drinking polluted water, causing hundreds of millions of cases of water-related diseases every year and over five million deaths. This amounted to ten times the number of people killed in wars worldwide."

I went on: "One of the most heartbreaking manifestations of the degradation of life on Earth was the decline of biodiversity, which was largely the result of human activities. And—Can you believe this? When Annie 'dropped by' my apartment back there/then just a couple of hours ago I happened to be rereading the September 2002 issue of *The Ecologist*. I had it in my hand when I was whisked over Here, and I've kept it with me. See? Here it is! In her article entitled 'State of the Planet' Matilda Lee reports '50–100 species are vanishing each day—10,000 times faster than natural extinction rates; faster than at any time in the last 65 million years.'[1] Actually, it was probably just after reading this article that I began howling so loudly that Annie heard me and came running!"

"So Here we are again!" the three of us all exclaimed together. We were laughing and crying at the same time.

Glancing at Annie, I couldn't resist commenting: "Lucky Annie! You weren't even born yet when Kate crossed over to Lost and Found. She was carrying you in utero." Perhaps there was a slightly annoyed tone in my voice, which would be resented by my listener.

Annie's astute reply confirmed my suspicion. "It is not my fault that I missed out on all that awful stuff, Mary, as you know very well," replied Annie. She gave me a sharp impish look. "And wasn't it you, Mary, who Named envy as one of the 'deadly sins of the fathers'?"

I was remorseful. "You're right," I said. "But I am deeply glad that you were spared, Annie. I am also grateful that Kate and I were able to help prepare the way for you and your contemporaries. Perhaps I'm still grumpy from my Transtemporal travel and am suffering from a sort of jet lag."

Annie gave me an odd look. "Jet lag?" she asked. Kate laughed at the anachronism. "I think we had this same time-warped discussion back in 2048 BE," she remarked. "Let's just go on. No need to repeat tedious explanations, right?" The squirrel, Annie's devoted friend, who had been waving her tail in my face in a rather insulting manner during this recent interchange, resumed eating her nuts.

I attempted a brief speech. "I don't know if you can even guess how thankful I am to all you Future Foresisters and Forefamiliars for your support, especially throughout recent years," I said. "There's one especially vivid Memory that has stayed with me since my last visit here in 2048 BE. I was sitting with many of you on Lost and Found beach. Innumerable animals had come along with us, and we were engaged in intense discussion. Remember?"

"We sure do!" exclaimed Annie and Kate—who were Now joined by a growing number of Lost and Found animals and women who had rushed over to our picnic and Re-membering session.

"It was then that you made your absolutely Stunning comment, Annie, which gave me and many Other women Hope during the past seven years back there/then," I said. "I have your words memorized, and they are printed in *Quintessence,* as you know."

"I just happen to have a copy of the 2048 BE edition with me," said Annie. Everyone laughed, and Kate commented on her daughter's "modesty." Not at all deterred by this friendly ridicule, Annie stood up, holding the book. "You are probably referring to my comment which is on page 236," she remarked.

After I nodded in agreement, Annie read in a strong, clear voice the following words:

"I'd like to get back to our original discussion of how we, as your Future Foresisters, can help you and your 'Cronies' Now," I said. "I guess it would be helpful if we communicate the fact that you are not a cognitive minority, as you may have imagined yourselves to be. After all, we are Here, as are Foresisters of more ancient patriarchal times and from the Archaic Past. Seen in this wide Transtemporal context, you belong to the cognitive *majority*."[2]

Annie then closed her copy of *Quintessence* and took a deep bow in my direction.

As she briskly made her way back to her place on the grass, the women, monkeys, and seals in the audience signaled their approval with loud applause. Various Other creatures meowed, barked, howled, oinked, mooed, bleated, roared, neighed, hissed, chirped, trilled, and whistled. Three large hens cackled. Two kookaburras laughed.

The laughter was contagious. Almost uncontrollably, we women laughed with them. After a Moment of calm silence, we Re-Called our great celebration on Lost and Found beach several years before, when we all Realized that the animals belong to— and are—the cognitive majority, together with plants, rocks, planets, stars, angels—and all Biophilic beings.

"It was then that the animals made it clear that our souls' work is their souls' work too," said Annie. "And it was the animals who announced that we have already won. Remember how we all telepathically heard and joined in their chorus, singing 'We *have* overcome!'

"These are all ecstatic and vivid Memories from 2048 BE," Annie continued. "But, Mary, I am extremely curious to know more about your own experiences and perceptions of life back there/then between 1998 and 2006 archetypal deadtime."

"I'm glad you are pressing me on this issue of communication, Annie," I replied. "I do feel strange about the fact that I have not been Here in this way for a while, but as you know, that is just a detail. In the most essential ways we are always in communication. We are always Present to each other. As Future Foresisters you draw us (my Cronies and me) into your electromagnetic field. And you yourSelves are affected by Foresisters of the Past."

"Right on!" said Kate. "And that raises some issues that I think it's important to clarify."

"OK. Let's get started!" I said, with my usual bluntness, while I offered a small bite of cake to the appreciative squirrel.

"How about a short break before we begin?" asked Annie, jumping up from her place on the grass. We all began to move and stretch. Even the snakes and turtles seemed to be doing their own kind of aerobics.

As we stretched our legs and chatted briefly, there was a general sense of excitement and anticipation. Some birds chattered among themselves and a few monkeys began swinging from the trees. A huge white mare reared up on her hind legs and neighed loudly.

"To each her own mode of Self-expression!" laughed Kate.

"I'll drink to that!" said Annie, sipping from a bottle of wine that was being passed around.

The number and variety of Anonyma Network women engaged in this conversation increased. I recognized several immediately. Among them I spotted Sung Hee, Myoko, and Nassrin, with whom I'd had great conversations during the memorable visits in 2048 BE. We all rushed over to greet each other. Next, Anowa, Annie's fiery friend of African descent, came sauntering over, characteristically carrying a notebook and pen.

"Hi, Anowa!" I said. "Still the impassioned scholar, I see!"

"Absolutely!" Anowa agreed, waving her notebook and smiling broadly.

"You have no idea, Mary!" interrupted Annie. "You'll have to see the mountains of notebooks and manuscripts she has filled with her research and reflections on the life and influence of Sojourner Truth. We had to build a special structure to house her library and writings over the past five years."

"Aw shucks!" laughed Anowa. "Ain't I a genius?"

"See, she's coy and modest, just like me," said Annie. "But honestly, Mary, you've written repeatedly about Elemental Feminist Genius. So what can you expect? Of course we have big heads!"

"Right! We raised a whole generation of Bigheads Here," said Sophie, Anowa's mother, who came along walking arm in arm with Kate. The two friends had made the Original Voyage over to Lost and Found Continent together in 2018 BE and were inseparable ever after, as were their daughters.

I was thrilled then at the familiar sight of the Wondrous Wolf Fenrir, the Super Natural Background Animal who was the Familiar/Graceful Friend of Annie whom I had first met in 2048. Fenrir came loping over to me, joyously swishing her beautiful tail. I felt greatly honored when she licked my face and allowed me to put my arms around her neck.[3] At the sight of Annie's Wolf-Friend, my own Feline Familiars, Cottie and her Foresisters (my Forefamiliars), Wild Cat and Aille Og—who had sneaked along behind me on this quick trip to Lost and Found Continent—scampered out from their hiding place behind a nearby bush. Then all four of these Spirited Animals immediately danced around together, licking each Other joyously.

At a signal from Annie, everyone took her place on the grass and breathlessly waited for our next discussion to begin.

CHAPTER SEVEN

A Transtemporal Exchange
of Information and
Strategic Discussion

"Kate," I began, "I seem to be on the verge of asking you an important question, but it is really difficult to articulate."

"Well, fire ahead anyway," she said, with an encouraging nod.

So I plunged in. "You remember that during one of our 2048 BE encounters you revealed that our lives were partially contemporaneous 'back then' in archetypal deadtime. I knew that you were a young woman who was interested in Feminist philosophy and had read some of my work with great eagerness, but we had never met. From what you said, I got the idea that you were about eighteen years old when I was completing the writing of *Quintessence* in Boston in 1998 a.d."

Kate, who was looking rather excited, said, "Yes, and in that same year, since I was interested in the history of Radical Feminist thought, I read the original edition of your first Feminist book, *The Church and the Second Sex*, which was published in 1968. It was quite an experience. I remember it well! I was in my freshman year in college. My friends and I tried to get you to come and speak at our school during that academic year (1998–99), but it seems that didn't work out for you."

Kate's gaze seemed to wander, as if she were staring at something far away. Then she said: "It didn't work out for me either, because in the course of that academic year, after I became aware that I was pregnant with Annie, I joined with some friends to form a network which we called 'Anonyma.' We took off on a Quantum Leaping Journey which led us to our Dis-covery of Lost and Found Continent!"

I was Stunned and confused by Kate's brief allusion to her Time-traveling adventures, but my attention was drawn to Anowa, who appeared to be calculating while scribbling figures in her notebook. "I get it!" she said loudly.

I started to say, "Well, I don't." However, I decided to continue with my narrative. "The fall of 1998 marked the beginning of my Final conflict with Boston College. It's interesting that this liberation from the confines of academentia began to happen at the same time as your Lusty Leap to Lost and Found Continent and the Biophilic Era."

"Sounds to me like an A-mazing Transtemporal Synchronicity," exclaimed Kate.

"It certainly does!" I agreed.

Following a brief pause, Annie asked me, "So what happened next, Mary?"

"Well," I answered, "by the winter of 1999 I was under assault—not for the first time—by the administration of Boston College. Those who followed my history with that institution recalled that I was first fired in 1969 because of *The Church and the Second Sex*, which my employers found upsetting."

Kate picked up the thread. "Weren't there lots of student demonstrations on your behalf in '69 as well as teach-ins and petitions about your case? Oh yes, and weren't most of the demonstrators male students? Why was that?"

"The reason for that was clear. Virtually all of my students in the late 1960s were males." Anticipating her next question, I added, "You see, the Jesuit administration at Boston College did not admit women to the College of Arts and Sciences before 1970. Women were restricted to the School of Nursing and the School of Education. I hadn't realized that fact when I accepted the job offer from BC to teach courses in A&S in 1966. I really enjoyed teaching those young men, though."

"They must have been very appreciative," said Kate. "I think that when they demonstrated and petitioned on your behalf they were also demonstrating what they had learned in your classes. They were publicly and colorfully asking whether their university was a place for the free exchange of ideas, or whether it was enclosed by the church. During those months of public actions and the attendant publicity, you were recognized as a cause célèbre and a symbol of academic freedom."

"Well, Kate, it appears that you learned the history very well," I remarked. "My question to you is: Where did you learn all this? You stated that you—uh—'took off' for Lost and Found Continent during your freshman year in college."

"Sure I did," Kate responded. "But that was in the fall of 1998. I found a number of newspaper clippings from the late '60s about your history at BC, and they were good sources of information. So also was your 'Autobiographical Preface to the 1975 Edition of The Church and the Second Sex,' as well as your 1992 autobiographical work, Outercourse."

"So, you're well informed in many dimensions, Kate," I commented wryly.

"I take that statement as a signal to go on," said Kate. "So your students' protests and the enormous publicity which they generated—together with the widespread influence of The Church and the Second Sex—resulted in victory for you in the summer of 1969. The newspapers said that you were promoted to the rank of associate professor and awarded tenure that summer. That certainly was a tumultuous time for you, Mary, wasn't it? Did that experience change your thinking?"

"Yes, absolutely, it did, Kate! It radicalized me profoundly. Although that was a great victory, I had come to see through the grim grasp of patriarchy, not only at Boston College but at all universities and throughout society. As I wrote in 1975:

> My concern was no longer limited to 'equality' in the church or anywhere else. I did not really care about unimaginative reform but instead began dreaming new dreams of a women's revolution. This was becoming a credible dream, because a community of sisterhood was coming into being, into be-ing. In the hearing/healing presence of these sisters I had grown ready to try writing/speaking New Words."[1]

Kate looked at me intensely. "Well, your dream of a women's revolution was Realized, at least to a great extent, wasn't it?"

"Sure, Kate," I said. "And it is still being Realized by many, as we both know. On a day-by-day, year-by-year level, though, it wasn't so simple. In 1970 Boston College began to admit women to its College of Arts and Sciences. I knew there would be further battles. The university continued to be threatened by my books and speeches, not to mention my Feminist philosophy and ethics courses, and my policy since the early '70s of teaching women and men in separate sections for those courses. So they continued to harass me for three more decades, but I had a lot of fun fighting them back."

Kate pursued her own train of thought. "But surely those three decades held many traumatic experiences for you. From what I've read I know that you were constantly under attack by the administration, even though you had many loyal student supporters—female and male—over those years, and always managed to win, and to have fun, as you said."

"That's right, Kate!" I responded. "But in '99, exactly thirty years after my first struggle, I was disappeared from my job at Boston College, where I'd been teaching since 1966."

Kate stared at me in horror. "How in the world could that have happened?" she gasped.

"By that time, Kate, the political/social/intellectual climate in America was infested by negative, greedy, power-mongering forces. The extreme right-wing republicans were taking over. To use a trite but apt phrase, 'the times had changed.' I could not have known back at the time of my celebrated victory in 1969 that, after thirty more years of fights and triumphs at that institution, another series of events would happen—bizarrely comparable to the original scenario. But I did know throughout the intervening years that my task was to Survive and Thrive on the Boundary of that university, consistently refusing them the false loyalty they tried to demand of me."

I raved on, "At both of these times of crisis my identity as a university professor at Boston College and indeed the possibility of continuing my life's work were being targeted for destruction. In the later attack, a potentially lethal attempt was made to throw me off balance—to destroy my capacity for proprioception, that is, 'reception of stimuli produced within the organism.' In other words, I was being challenged to find a New sense of balance, a New Sense of where I am in Space."

Kate was wide-eyed. "Hold on, Mary. You're racing ahead of me. Could you be more specific? What happened, exactly?"

"Right you are, Kate," I said. Catching my breath, I set forth some facts. "On the afternoon of December 8, 1998, I received a frantic phone call from the chair of the theology department. I could hardly listen to him, since I was rushing to finish my class preparation and then dash over to teach my 4:30 class. So I asked him to call me again the next day. On the following day I learned from him that a male undergraduate student who had attempted in September to register in my class 'Introduction to Feminist Ethics,' without having the prerequisites, would be in my class in January 1999, with or without my consent, and whether or not he had completed the course prerequisites. The chair, who sounded nervous and terrified, hastily explained that this student was

backed by an ultra-right law firm in Washington, D.C., known as
the Center for Individual Rights (CIR). Citing Title IX, the federal
legislation intended to provide *women* with equal access to educational resources, the student, a pro-bono client of the CIR, was
threatening a lawsuit against Boston College for sex discrimination!"

Kate was stunned. "But Mary, how could they have pulled that
off? As you know, I was a college student at that time (just before
I 'took off' for Lost and Found Continent). I was quite aware of
the meaning and importance of Title IX for women's equality. I
assumed that almost all educated people knew what that meant!"

I attempted to explain this instance of reversal. "The CIR fellows used Duane, who was a leader of the 'Young Republicans' on
campus. They were cynically taking advantage of the conditions of
heightened right-wing backlash, including the climate of doublethink and reversal, which of course they promoted. For about
twenty-five years I'd had a classroom policy of teaching women
and men separately in my Feminist Ethics classes. I developed this
method during the early 1970s, after I saw the dulling of women's
participation that occurred in mixed classes. Of course, I never refused to teach a student, female or male, who expressed interest
and had completed the course prerequisites."

"It's clear that you were acting in accordance with the intent of
Title IX," said Kate.

"Of course I was," I said. "In fact, the duplicitous CIR openly
opposed Title IX, calling it 'one of feminism's sacred cows.' They
specifically targeted individual radicals and feminist initiatives,
such as the federal Violence Against Women Act."

"It's obvious that Boston College knuckled under to that right-
wing law firm," said Anowa.

"I'd say it's also obvious that they were more than willing to
knuckle under!" exclaimed Annie. "It seems that the CIR tried to
help BC to achieve what they had tried and failed to do in thirty
years of sustained effort."

"Well, yes," I said. "But the important point is that they tried
and, on the deepest level, failed again. Here's what happened: In a

stunning and underhanded move BC agreed to a settlement with the CIR in the fall of 1998, before a single paper was filed, and without any notice to me. I later saw a copy of the CIR letter to the president of Boston College, which, curiously, was dated October 16, which happens to be my birthday. Their secret demands included the stipulation that the student would be registered in my spring 1999 Feminist Ethics class despite his lack of the Women's Studies prerequisite and without my consent. This was not unconnected to the fact that BC was under increasing pressures to conform to Vatican rulings and affirm its own orthodoxy and fidelity to catholic teachings, while at the same time pretending to champion an open environment and academic freedom."

"It all sounds typically patriarchal—so slimy and convoluted and basely deceptive! Yuk!" exclaimed Nassrin, who was usually very quiet.

Some ducks began quacking. Their quacks sounded to me like a series of "Yuks." Apparently I was not alone in my odd perception, because a group of women began laughing and then broke into a chorus of "Yukking."

"Sounds like a band of Yuk-Ducks!" commented Sophie. "Maybe they should call themselves 'The Yuk-Duck Chorus.'" Fenrir howled her approval.

"Enough of this Silliness!" announced Kate. "Mary must continue her grim account."

I went on. "By January 1999 I came to the conclusion that the best way to avoid the trap of being forced to admit the impostor into my class would be to take a leave of absence for that semester and begin work on my next book."

I was interrupted by loud cheers. I then continued presenting the facts to my increasingly rowdy but still attentive audience. "The administration at first appeared amenable to granting my request for a leave but soon used this proposal as an opportunity for luring me into 'meetings' in the office of the Vice President for 'Human Resources,' who enjoyed a reputation for employing Inquisitorial tactics. The ostensible purpose of the required meeting

with this fellow was to discuss the conditions of my leave. My attendance was presented as a *sine qua non* for obtaining the leave. Despite my misgivings and under protest, I agreed to participate in two 'meetings' in January, in the desperate hope of obtaining my leave. I realized that the situation was treacherous. It smelled worse than just 'fishy.' It smelled bad."

At this point in my account my Feline Friends, who were crouching near me, began hissing slowly. Cottie, who was in attack mode, leaped forward, Wild-eyed, charging at something that was invisible—to me at any rate—but whose negative presence could be Sensed by all of us. Her attack worked as an exorcism, and "something" appeared to slither and glide away from our Space. Fenrir Howled.

"I am feeling chilled," said Annie.

"I can't seem to stop shivering," said Anowa.

"Mary, please hurry and finish your account," Kate said tersely.

I continued. "In a panic during one of these meetings, I must have blurted out something like 'I'd rather resign than teach under these conditions,' and they jumped at this chance to take me at my word. It soon became evident in the course of these meetings that the administration had no intention of granting me a straightforward leave of absence but was intent upon forcing me to sign a 'retirement agreement.' The 'agreement' contained a lengthy and convoluted 'confidentiality clause'—in other words, a gag order."

I was interrupted by a resounding cacophonous interlude from "The Yuk-Duck Chorus."

When the Yukking faded I forged ahead: "In the face of some blatant attempts at psychological arm-twisting by that administrator I refused adamantly to sign any such 'agreement.'"

Again there was an interruption, this time consisting of meows, cheers, howls, oinks, roars, moos, neighs, barks, whistles, trills, cackles, and more. Overwhelmed by this wonderful show of support, I thanked everyone. "Thank you! Thank you! Thank you!" I said.

Kate stood up and signaled for silence. She nodded to me to continue.

"In February 1999 I began in earnest to search for a good lawyer. My efforts were rewarded. I found a civil rights attorney who was a Feminist activist, who agreed to represent me in my struggle against Boston College. I filed a lawsuit against the university for breach of contract, for constructive discharge, and for violation of my academic freedom and tenure rights."

Anowa spoke out. "But you knew that the legal system was hopelessly phallocratic!"

"Of course I did!" I yelled. "That's why I always had used Other ways of fighting back. But the Time of great massive demonstrations was over. The late nineties was the beginning of a period of dulled-out, draining, deadheaded daddydom. So the weapon at hand was their paralyzing patriarchal legal system, which I hated."

The women groaned. Cats and snakes hissed. A group of monkeys screeched. Fenrir bared her teeth and snarled.

I carried on. "In the spring of that year the administration continued its outrageous assault. BC brazenly and deceitfully proclaimed that I had resigned. One administrator came to a meeting of the theology department (from which I was absent) and publicly announced this disinformation. My name and course listings were removed from the university catalog and preregistration materials for the academic year 1999–2000. All this was done without notice to me and without the due process guaranteed to me as a faculty member with tenure."

"I'm beginning to feel those chills again," said Annie. Her comment was echoed by others, who seemed to be unconsciously huddling closer together.

"It was not until the end of the twentieth century, the time when the ultraconservative takeover of power in the US and in the catholic church was rapidly encroaching, that they reached the point of savagely and illegally disappearing me. The tenure that the BC administration had grudgingly granted to me in 1969 in response to the demand from thousands of their students, alumni, and other concerned persons was flagrantly violated by the administration. BC broke the promise made by the university to their students, as well as the promise inherent in tenure itself. They believed that they could get away with this ruthless act. I could not let them get away with it."

The animals and women stood up. After a Moment of silence Sophie said simply, "And we Here on Lost and Found did not let them get away with it!"

"Oh, absolutely! Thank you," I said. "Of course, you were Present as Magnetic Attractors, Guiding me—Guiding and Guarding all of us—in our pursuit of the Final Cause."

"Will you say more about how that worked itself out?" asked Kate. "I mean, what about the experiences involved, the specifics of losses and victories?"

"I'll be happy to describe these," I said. "But first I want to acknowledge the context of such struggles for Radical Feminist Amazons. First, as you know, I am aware that I am at the center of this story/adventure insofar as it is my own story. As Amazonian Adventurers we are all at the center of our own stories. Yet they all overlap, as we move into participation in the powers of the Goddess Nemesis, Who is the true Center of our converging adventures. Her work, which is also our work, is Elemental disruption of the patriarchal balance of terror. At the same time, it is Passionate Spinning/Spiraling of Archaic threads of Gynergy.

"Now, in response to your question about my own experience of being disappeared from Boston College in the spring of 1999, and the atrocities leading up to this, I can say that it was a compound traumatic event. To be more precise, it involved a complex series of shocks, each of which had multiple layers that interacted with each other. I could not understand immediately all that was happening. I Sensed that it had something in common with gang rape. To explain this intuition I Now call upon a word from the *Wickedary*, namely, *rapism*. What they perpetrated against me was an act of *rapism*, which means

> the fundamental ideology and practice of patriarchy, characterized by invasion, violation, degradation, objectification, and destruction of women and nature; the fundamental paradigm of racism, classism, and all other oppressive -isms.[2]

"Since this manifestation of rapism was not simply physical, it was hard at first to Name its multiple levels of invasion, violation, degradation, and destruction, and the horror of this. These levels can be glimpsed only when one recognizes that I was not the only target of this maneuver."

"I get it," said Anowa. "By invading and violating your class-room and taking away your job, they were trying to shut you up and destroy the possibility of Women's Space at that school—as far as their tentacles could reach. Yuk!"

As if on cue, "The Yuk-Duck Chorus" started Yukking. As be-fore, Kate assumed the role of maintaining order. "Quiet!" she shouted. After the women in the Chorus settled down, the ducks in the pond continued to carry on. "You too!" she yelled at them.

When silence was restored, Anowa boldly raised her hand, waving at me imploringly.

"What do *you* think, Anowa? " I said.

"I was just about to make one of my most important points, when all the—uh—noise began," she said emphatically. "I want to point out that your Women Only classes appear to me to have been like anticipations of what we have Here at Lost and Found Continent all the time! And without the disgustingly hostile en-vironment of 'BC.' Did you have something like foreglimpses of Lost and Found during those twenty-five years?"

"Well, Anowa, that raises important questions about Trans-temporal understanding and travel, doesn't it?" I responded. "I didn't make my first Voyage to Lost and Found until 1998 a.d., when Annie invoked me. Of course, it was then 2048 BE on Lost and Found. I must have had some subliminal 'foreglimpses,' as you so nicely put it. There are traces and signs of such subliminal knowledge, but I don't think I can answer the question further than that."

I continued: "I've been wondering about how the Anonyma Network members—our Future Foresisters—have been pulling us along, Magnetizing us. This Magical Interaction is part of the Magnetic Magic that Annie wrote about in her Preface to the 2048 Edition of *Quintessence.* Just thinking about it makes me feel quite spacey."

At that Moment, everyone gasped. I didn't know what all the gasping was about until I was told later that after Anowa's ques-tion, I Momentarily disappeared. I recall hearing someone say:

"This is exactly like what happened at the end of her visits in 2048 BE. Annie, especially, found that disconcerting." Then I heard Annie's plaintive voice. "Yes, it is disconcerting. There is always so much more to say!"

It seems that after Annie's comment I immediately reappeared and was seen sitting in the same place as if nothing had happened. I heard another gasp and innocently asked what was going on.

"You tell us!" said Annie. "Don't you know it is very unnerving when you suddenly leave like that? You did that in 2048 BE. But this time you left and then suddenly came back!"

I apologized profusely and tried to explain. "You see, what was going on for me was that first I was puzzling over Anowa's question, and so I became sort of lost in thought, as it were. Then I was suddenly shaken by hearing Annie's voice complaining: 'There is so much more to say.' I was thinking specifically about the importance of Women's Space and how much I long to be Here with you. So I guess that thought and that longing sort of snapped me back, I mean, ahead. So . . . Hi!" I added feebly.

We all sort of laughed and cried at the same time. Fenrir simply trotted over to me and put her paw on my shoulder.

Anowa said what we all were thinking. "Fenrir just made the most enlightening demonstration and comment about Women's Space. She's saying: 'It's the animals who make it possible!'"

After much appreciative roaring, mooing, cheering, snarling, twittering, et cetera, we all stood up and stretched, getting ready for our next Big Discussion.

Chapter Eight

Women's Space and Amazon Grace

After an hour or so of relaxation we settled down again for the next phase of our Transtemporal discussion. "I'd like to continue our discussion of Women's Space," said Kate.

"All right. Let's go!" I said. "As I wrote in *Quintessence*, our work is both envisioning and creating the world we have been envisioning. As I understood Women's Space back there/then, this Space/Time is a locus for Realizing such a twofold project. It is of its nature prophetic. And you, my Foresisters of the Archaic Future, are furthering this work."

"And as we all cast ourSelves farther Out," continued Kate, "we Realize more fully our true identity as Outcasts. As Outcasts from patriarchy/phallocracy/fooldom/snooldom we break open the casts/castes in which the fools/snools have enclosed women."

"Yes," said Sophie, "and we Run and Leap far, far away and Find ourSelves Here, on Lost and Found."

"And we know When and How and Where to Leap, because the Final Cause, or End, causes by attraction," said Annie. "We understand from our own experience that the Final Cause is first in the order of intentionality. So the End is really the Beginning."

"Right, Annie," I said. "The End makes itself Present to us by magnetic attraction. When we experience the attractive energy of the End, we find the will and the means to achieve it. It is not necessary to focus obsessively on the means because the power of this attraction has a magical effect. It manifests the truth of the adage 'Where there's a will there's a way.'"

"Oh, yes!" broke in Kate. "Concretely, this means that Things begin to Happen. Books literally jump off shelves. The right helpers just happen to show up when needed. Synchronicities abound. Seeing a particular film suggests layers of ideas and possible actions that previously were hidden. The world shimmers with heretofore unsuspected messages and meanings. Friendships are formed and fired. Creative endeavors flame out and flourish. We begin to Re-member the experience of Happiness."

"What is most exciting in this process of Realizing the End is that we begin to Sense its Presence not only as magnetic attractor but also as morphic attractor," I said. "That is, we begin to understand that it engenders what Rupert Sheldrake has called 'morphic fields.'"[1]

"Well, you continue to use Sheldrake as a springboard, and that's fine with me," said Kate. "As you know, Mary, we managed to bring some of his works to Lost and Found Continent, having been motivated by your suggestion, so we can follow through on the references. We understand that you Spin off from his work at times, as well as those of other male authors such as Aristotle and Aquinas, while always giving due credit. This is characteristic of your work as a Radical Feminist Pirate: righteously ripping off knowledge that has been stolen from women, as you explain in your intellectual autobiography, *Outercourse*."

"Thanks, Kate, for being so attentive," I said. "Yes, that is exactly what I do. I try to be scrupulously honest in identifying these sources, which I look upon as secondary sources, and then developing—and sometimes altering—the ideas as they help us to unfold our own understanding of the Archaic Past and Future."

"I'm impatient to hear more about this," said Kate.

"Great!" I replied. "To Leap back to Sheldrake's theory, then, I will begin by paraphrasing and quoting from his Glossary to *The Presence of the Past*. In his definition of *morphic field* he writes:

> The term *morphic field* includes morphogenetic, behavioral, social, cultural, and mental fields. Morphic fields are shaped and stabilized by morphic resonance from previous similar morphic units, which were under the influence of fields of the same kind. They consequently contain a kind of cumulative memory and tend to become increasingly habitual.[2]

"You see, Kate," I said, "the definition—though Sheldrake most likely could not have thought of this—applies beautifully to our inheritance from the Foresisters of the Past, who were 'under the influence of fields of the same kind.' But there is a problem."

"Let me guess," said Kate. "Does it have something to do with the word *previous* in the definition?"

"Right on!" I replied. "Nothing is mentioned about the important causal role of the Future. This would appear to leave no room for the influence of Lost and Found Continent. The problem is even more explicit in the Glossary definition of *morphic resonance*. Sheldrake explains this as

> the influence of previous structures of activity on subsequent similar structures of activity organized by morphic fields. Through morphic resonance, formative causal influences pass through or across space and time, and these influences are assumed not to fall off with distance in space or time, but they come only from the past.[3]

"So there you have it! It would seem that you cannot influence us," I said with a conspiratorial grin. "I must just be hallucinating about the influence of you Future Foresisters."

"Well, it does apparently leave us inhabitants of Lost and Found Continent pretty much out of the picture, doesn't it?" queried Kate, with a perplexed smile.

"I wouldn't worry about it," I said reassuringly. "After all, we have met and Here we are, Now! The possibilities of mutual creation are virtually unlimited."

Kate seemed to have a dawning realization. "Yes. And I am having another insight about all this," she exclaimed. "The irksome thing about the passage from Sheldrake that you just read was the way emphasis is placed on the past, as in his statement that the formative causal influences come only from the past. That sounds like a one-way street if we hear it only superficially. But . . ."

I rudely interrupted. "Oh, I think I get what you're driving at, Kate," I said. "If we choose to hear that passage about morphic resonance in our own context, we can hear the word *past* as meaning Archaic Past. Since our Sense of Time is not linear, but Spiraling, it is always enlightening to reflect upon the Archaic Future as coming from the Prepatriarchal Past. So the Archaic Future Re-Calls (calls back, calls ahead) that Past. And it Re-Names the Past and Re-energizes that Past, Re-Newing its causal force, Re-Causing its causality."

Kate nodded. "Yes, and it is our shared participation in that Past that makes possible our mutual Gynergizing influence." She paused and looked at me quizzically. "I wonder what you were just thinking, Mary," she said. "You have that 'spacey' look that has become familiar to your friends here on Lost and Found Continent. What's up?"

"Oh, I was just thinking about the very last sentence of the Epilogue to *The Presence of the Past,* where Sheldrake writes:

We shall sooner or later have to give up many of our old habits of thought and adopt new ones: habits that are better adapted to life in a world that is living in the presence of the past—and is also living in the presence of the future, and open to continuing creation.[4]

"Funny that he was inspired to write that at the very end of the book," I said.

"Yes," Kate agreed. "And it's even funnier that we are sitting Here discussing it. We seem to be doing quite well in adopting 'New habits of thought,' as we sit and chat on Lost and Found Continent."

We both Be-Laughed in Self-congratulation. Our Be-Laughing Re-Sounded in Great Spiraling Waves Out into the farthest reaches of the Universe. It is Re-Sounding Now.

CHAPTER NINE

THE SELF-DESTRUCTION OF PATRIARCHY AND THE RE-EMERGENCE OF FEMALE POWER

As I ABRUPTLY ARRIVED BACK AT MY DESK in archetypal dead-time everything was in its usual disorder. My cup of coffee had gone cold and my glass of water had become lukewarm, and the papers and books were in disarray, as always. It seemed as if I had just been out briefly on an errand. I joked to my Feline Familiar, Cottie, that I was beginning to feel like an Errand Messenger from the Realm of Lost and Found. She yawned.

I was in a State of Shock, naturally, knowing that I really had been Way Out, participating in a mode of Be-ing that is peculiar to those who have Dis-covered Lost and Found Continent. I can look forward to further trips, of course. But there is such a feeling of having gone "plop" into this dreary world whenever I return.

Ah, but here's the magical, wondrous thing: My life in a.d. changes incrementally with the accumulation of these Far Out experiences. I am immeasurably enriched by them, by my Memories of them. Having entered an Other morphic field, I carry it back with me to this dreary dimension—which never was entirely dreary because there always were "foreglimpses."

But the Memories of these Adventures are not merely some passive baggage that I carry with me: They have lives of their own. They interact with each other. Weaving a kind of glistening Web of energy, they shine on and transform everything, so that even common things display their participation in this dancing Web.

Many women have experiences of be-ing in this dimension of energy, which they experience as different from "ordinary" life. Often the experiences seem like Memories of an Other world in which colors are different, smells are different, sounds, tastes, textures are different.

The Memories often are dim in the sense of seeming far away. They are difficult to Name. If we employ a name to describe them, we know that it is not quite adequate. We may name something on "this level," but we are overstretching its power when we apply it to "that dimension." One could use the word *blue*, for example, to name a color, but the word fails. Or almost fails. It may work for the speaker who has had this "Other" experience, to trigger a Memory of that richer, subtler reality, but it cannot really convey the meaning she intends. Perhaps she can speak of the problem of Naming it, however, and thereby trigger indirectly some comparable Memory in the person to whom she is speaking.

It is fruitful to see this range of meaning in connection with the scholastic philosophers' explanation of the "analogy of being" (*analogia entis*), which I interpret to mean "analogy of be-ing." In the scholastic tradition, in this analogy the analogates are said to be "simply different and somewhat the same." This means that the difference is greater than the sameness. Thus the rock is being (be-ing); the tree is being (be-ing); the human is being (be-ing); ultimate reality is being (be-ing). However, the difference in the meaning of being/be-ing is greater than the sameness among these realities.

My experience with Naming the color range with the same word, e.g., green, is comparable. It is noteworthy that this experience occurred long before I studied scholastic philosophy, which tells me that the insight is intuitive, not contrived. It is, in fact, shockingly real knowledge, like the intuition of be-ing. For this reason it is difficult to communicate and retain in a foregrounded world.

The strange and almost elusive problem of a kind of amnesia arises. When one has such an Otherworld experience she senses this danger of amnesia in herSelf. She sometimes fears a loss of a particular Memory and prays that the universe will help her remember, or she asks the Memory itself to stay with her. She expresses a Hope that she will not forget.

Sometimes she does forget, perhaps for years. The overcoming of such amnesia is what Lost and Found Continent is all about.

Shortly after I wrote the preceding paragraphs I heard from my friend Ann Marie Palmisciano, who told me that a strange word had popped into her mind very recently while she was doing her laundry.[1] The word was *cosmochromatic*. To my knowledge this word does not exist in any dictionary. It does exist on this page, however. Before that, it existed when Ann Marie first Heard it and again when we spoke about it. We were both startled by the Synchronicities involved in this revelatory event. *Cosmochromatic* is Stunningly apt for Naming the cosmic, multidimensional range of reality that can be signified by the name of a specific color.

In conversations with Ann Marie she has told me about a wonderful dictionary she inherited from her father. This dictionary is called *Webster's Complete Reference Dictionary and Encyclopedia*.[2] In that work, she encountered the word *chromotopsia*, therein defined as "a morbid state of vision in which objects appear in abnormal colors."

In the course of our conversation we concluded that *chromotopsia* would certainly characterize the quality of vision in the foregrounded/unreal state. Of course, we are trained not to notice the degradation of sense perception as well as the depravity of intellect, emotions, behaviors, social interactions, and "values" in this state.

All of these manifestations of degradation and depravity are interconnected. The abnormally glaring lights and colors of a TV set or shopping mall beckon us into the fake world they so aptly represent. They set us up for myriad encounters with pseudo-reality on the screen and in the mall. By lying to our senses, they lie to our minds, seducing us to mistake the unreal for the real.

The feelings/emotions of those so deceived become twisted. They learn to favor the phony. Bored with nature, they prefer to be surrounded by fake everything. They themselves begin to fake everything. They fake happiness. Fearing the knowledge of un-happiness, they practice the habit of forgetting happiness. Having lost it, they choose not to find it.

The victims of TV land and shopping mall hell, as well as meaningless "education" and jobs, are prime candidates for im-prisonment in totalitarian society. This was manifested in early-twenty-first century America by the plutocracy/oligarchy/oiligarchy which I shall simply Name *bushdom*.

Bushdom (bushdumb) began decades (perhaps millennia) before the reign of G. W. Bush, whose absence of Presence and breath-taking inanity suggest that he was not only unoriginal but un-questionably/unquestioningly a copy. The real question is: Copy of what? A procession of nothings, perhaps? The anality/banality brings to mind yet again Hannah Arendt's often quoted expres-sion "the banality of evil."

Despite the spread of the vacuous nonpresence which I Name *bushdom*, breakthroughs began to occur. The resistance to the US government's warmongering against Iraq as well as to nuclear threats around the globe, which had been building in the late 1990s and in the first years of the twenty-first century, was man-ifested in large peace demonstrations, especially throughout Eu-rope, the Middle East, Australia, and the US. A shift in public consciousness was becoming visible, tangible. There were signs that the critical mass required for effective resistance was becom-ing attainable.

I suggest that the primary obstacle to the attainment of critical mass is deadly distraction.

Before proceeding further, it is important to reflect further on *bushdom,* which is characterized by distraction. GW is a major distraction. He is essentially a distraction.

GW does not matter. He deflects attention from the problem. He is a decoy. This is precisely why Bush and *bushdom* are important. They are expansions of "the banality of evil." They give new shades of meaning to the term *phony.*

Here is the reason why so many people insist that they cannot bear the sight of dubya on television and feel compelled to turn off their sets when they hear *that voice.* If good is that which attracts, evil is that which disgusts and distracts.

Hitler and Mussolini failed to achieve the degree of horrifying absence which is projected by the selected president of the world's only remaining superpower, the nonelected resident of the white house.

It is not simply a case of an unpleasant personal appearance. TV screens and newspapers are full of ugly men's faces and bodies. Nor is it merely a grinding, irritating voice (think Kissinger). The GW phenomenon is that which radically repels by flagrantly flaunting absence of be-ing.

As I continued to dwell upon this thought, I recalled newspaper photos of the bush gang in Washington: Cheney, Rumsfeld, Powell, and—oh! Condoleezza Rice, the ultimate double token/double cross. I thought of the 2003 editorial in *The New York Times* on Bush's "war against women."[3] I thought of the millions of actual and potential victims of "weapons of mass destruction," not just members of the human species, but all species of living beings on Earth.

I heard in my mind a line in Adrienne Rich's poem "Hunger": "Quantify suffering, you could rule the world."[4]

"That's what it's all about!" I thought for the hundredth time. "They intend to finish the job for Hitler—a thousand times more efficiently and powerfully than Adolf could have managed to do it. They intend to rule and ruin the world!" I shouted this at Cottie, who was dozing sweetly on her green armchair. She woke up, giving me an annoyed glance. Alarmed at the slowness of my thought processes, she rolled over.

I slumped over my desk, dropping my head on my arms. I then raised my head and Howled.

Suddenly the door of my study swung open. In strode Kate, yelling: "Please stop that noise. We heard you on Lost and Found Continent. You woke us all up!"

I turned around and stared. Then I jumped up and hugged Kate. "You came all this way! Thank you. Thank you!" I exclaimed.

"It's not so far, as you know very well," she said. "Just a holler away."

"It's good to be reminded of that," I said. "We're all so drained back here—*bushed*, that is—to borrow a term from Emily Culpepper."

"Remember your own words about Hopping Hope," said Kate. "You can Hop out of this dreary dimension if you really want to. You don't have to let yourself be bushed around by arrogant snools."

At the sound of Kate's voice, Cottie suddenly Hopped up from her cozy green chair and landed on my desk, where she sat up sturdily, confirming Kate's words with her determined stare.

"You see, Cottie gets it!" exclaimed Kate, taking the cat's place on the green chair. "She's saying, 'Come back Here to your computer, Mary, and write. It's by your writing that you keep your Hope Hopping. It Hops from one woman to another, from one animal to another, from one dimension to another. This Hope is contagious!' Your Hopping/Writing is extremely important to Cottie and to us, Mary."

"Oh, I do know that is true, Kate!" I said. "That cat is constantly urging me on. She waits for hours on my desk chair, while I'm getting my act together before sitting down to work. And while I'm writing she often goes into what seems to be a kind of doze or trance, lying with her front paws outstretched, deeply in harmony with the vibrations that surround the process of writing. When she senses that I am pushing too late at night, trying to finish a section and becoming unproductive because of fatigue, she comes over and rubs against my legs, hinting that it's time to quit, have a snack, and go to bed. Back in 2003 when I was distracted from my own work by horrifying news about 'the war against terrorism,' that cat actually went on hunger strikes for days. I think she was trying to shock me into getting my priorities straight."

"Clearly she is a very special companion animal!" said Kate.

"She is an incredibly inspiring and encouraging partner in the creation of this book, Kate. I'd like to tell you about something astonishing that she did just a few days ago." I said this hesitantly, hoping that I was not sounding like an excessively proud parent.

"I'm all ears," responded my guest with a partially suppressed smile.

"Well, she had been sitting where you are, on the green chair. You can see that the chair is very close to the bookcase on your left."

Kate turned to examine the overfilled bookshelves. "I can see that the shelves are jam-packed with a wide variety of books. At first glance the volumes don't seem to be arranged in very strict categories," she commented.

"Right," I said. "And part of Cottie's genius is the ability to unscramble them. This talent was manifested just the other day, when suddenly this inquisitive cat hopped up onto the left arm of that chair, which brought her about even with the middle shelf. She began searching among the books there and paused when her nose was directly pointed at the spine of a nondescript paperback which I didn't immediately recognize. When I pulled it out I was amazed to see that it was *1984* by George Orwell—a book that has been on my mind for years but which apparently had been lost before she found it."

"Lost and Found!" Kate exclaimed. "Probably you should reread it right away."

I agreed. "I did open it immediately and read some lines about Oceania's war with Eastasia and/or Eurasia. These struck a familiar note, not only because I had read them before, but also because they were aptly descriptive of what human society is rapidly becoming in the early years of the twenty-first century. Orwell's book presents a horrifying picture of a world in which doublethink prevails, memory is destroyed, the capacity to reason is broken, and all genuine love, self-respect, loyalty, and hope for a real future are gone."

Kate's eyes flashed. "It certainly is a portentous book, but it would seem unlikely that such a dystopian novel could engender Hopping Hope. Come to think of it, though, I remember reading it 'back there/then' and subsequently feeling impelled to Leap toward an Other kind of Future. It helped drive me to reach Out toward the Archaic Future and search for Lost and Found Continent."

"That was a great Biophilic response to a necrophilic book, Kate," I said. "As you recall, the year 2048 BE was the year I first visited Lost and Found Continent. I remember that we all were acutely aware that '48 reverses '84. It was then that your audacious daughter Annie and I celebrated together the final defeat of Big Brother. It was Annie who proclaimed: 'He finally shriveled up and died ignominiously of his own inherent rottenness.' We congratulated ourSelves and all our Foresisters on this victory."

Kate laughed. "It's a great 'coincidence' that '48 reverses '84. And what a cosmic Synchronicity it was that we managed to bring out the 2048 BE Edition of *Quintessence* on Lost and Found Continent just in time for the publication of the book in Boston by Beacon Press. That made it possible for Beacon to include the 'Cosmic Comments and Conversations with the Author' that were written by Annie (whose pen name, of course, is Anonyma)."

Eager to push ahead with my discussion of Cottie's findings, I said, "Almost immediately after she pointed to *1984*, Cottie selected a second book for me from that shelf. This time she did not simply point with her nose. She actually picked at the book with her paw, partially dislodging it from its place. When I pulled it out I saw that this slender volume is entitled *Panhandling Papers*, that it is 'by Kady,' and that the beautiful drawing of Kady on the cover was done by Paula Gottlieb in 1981. The book, which was published in 1989, is beautifully made. It consists of 217 pages. The paper, the binding, and the print are of excellent quality. The back cover sports an excellent photo of Kady crouching with a cat at the Seneca Army Depot. The photographer is Barbara Adams, and the photo was copyrighted in 1983. *Panhandling Papers* was officially Self-published in 1989 by Kay Vandeurs (i.e., Kady). In sum, Kady's book is a labor of Wild Honesty, Courage, and Love."

"Cottie exhibited true Canniness in her selection of those two books," said Kate.

"Yes," I replied. "Comparing them is a remarkable experience. For example, I've been thinking about Winston's secret project in *1984* of writing a book against Big Brother. He had to write this book in secrecy, in a state of perpetual fear of being found out. This situation was plausible to the reader because of the context, which was 1984."

"But then," I continued, "as I read the words of Kady, I Remembered vividly the fact that in the foreground, every year is 1984 for women. The first essay in *Panhandling Papers*, which was written in 1979, contains the following lines: 'A journal is a notebook in which I write to mySelf in secret. The only time most women can speak honestly is in a secret notebook.'[5]

"Kady concludes that essay with the following paragraph:

> When we write in our journals, we are speaking silently and nobody hears. But now we begin to dare to read our journals aloud. We begin to find our voices. We begin to see, hear, say: "I am talking about 5 thousand years of slavery—my slavery, my mother's, her mother's—all the women in the world for generations and generations." Nobody knows what to do, and yet we are doing it. Millions of obscure women begin to dare to speak. Our pens are dangerous weapons. We pool our wisdom.[6]

"I pondered briefly in foolish amazement the fact that this essay was written 'only' twenty-six years ago. But then I Re-membered that the difference between women's condition in 1979 and in the early twenty-first century is not really so great. It might seem so, especially to privileged academics. But the reality is that—despite foreground changes—Big Brother still looms everywhere, and things are getting worse. The date is perpetually '1984' for women.

"An astonishing synchronicity began to reveal itself to me when I flipped back to the epigraph at the very beginning of Kady's book:

For those who follow their enthusiasms
into deep and treacherous waters
where they must struggle to keep from drowning—
before going down for the last time—
Your life flashed before you as a panorama—
Clutch your pen and write.
Go on and write, Fool, before your heart breaks!

written by
my grandmother Kate
a long time ago[7]

"So Kady's grandmother's name was Kate," I continued, "and Kate encouraged Kady and, by implication, all women, to write. When I read this I thought of my own grandmother, whose name also was Kate. The plot thickens. Browsing through the book, I learned that Kady identifies herSelf as follows:

My name is Kady daughter of Ann
daughter of Kate
daughter of Anna
daughter of Anna.[8]

"My mind raced back and ahead at the same time. I first thought of the fact that my own mother's name was/is Anna and that she was often called Ann for short. In that same instant I Re-Called the fact that my mother's mother's name was/is Kate and that my grandmother Kate's mother's name was/is Johanna. I then Re-membered that my mother's baptismal name was Johanna (after her grandmother) but, as she explained, she did not care much for that name and so she was called Anna—sometimes Ann. (In order to tease her, my father occasionally called her 'Josie.') My, how it all came together!

"In that Moment of Dis-covery of the odd synchronicity (Syn-Crone-icity) between Kady's genealogy and my own, my mind

was brought to focus on the genesis of the Anonyma Network—
the group of farseeing Foresisters who Dis-Covered Lost and
Found Continent in 2018 BE. The origins of this Network are described by Annie in her Preface to the 2048 BE Edition of *Quintessence* as follows:

> As a member of the Network, I choose to write under the noble
> name Anonyma, but my friends just call me Annie. My mother,
> whose name is Kate, was born in 1980.... From her earliest years
> she imbibed understanding of the Women's Movement from *her*
> mother, Johanna. My grandmother, Johanna, who was born in
> 1942, participated wholeheartedly in the Movement."[9]

Turning to my Transtemporal visitor, I said, "So you see, Kate,
how compounded these odd 'coincidences' are."

"And you had not read Kady's book before you wrote *Quintessence?*" queried Kate. "I mean, perhaps that could have influenced
you."

"If I did, I have no conscious memory of having read it," I
responded.

Kate was looking at me intently. "I'm beginning to make some
sense of all this," she said. "You told me that your experience with
Cottie finding Orwell's and Kady's books occurred in late February or early March of 2003 a.d. That was just a few weeks before
the hideous war initiated by the Bush administration against Iraq
actually happened. Isn't that right?"

"Yes," I replied, trying to get the dates straight in my mind.
"You know, I have been horribly distracted from my writing by the
grotesque media coverage of the war. It has had a kind of hypnotic
effect, and it is addictive. So you came just in time, Kate. You are
jolting me out of the state of distraction."

"That's good," said Kate. "As you have repeatedly pointed out in
your books, phallocracy's wars and media do have just that effect—
cutting off women from our own Selves, our own work, and creativity. So Now I think it's time for us to pull some threads together.
It seems to me that when you brought up the subject of the 'coinci-

dental' Naming of Kady's genealogy and your own and then linked all this with the Names of your friends on Lost and Found Continent you were describing an amazingly intense sense of temporal convergence. You were expressing the intertwining of Past, Present, and Future. And your keen awareness of such convergence seems to be connected with the Bush gang's cruel and unjust war."

"Our awareness of our own Positive Convergence can be triggered by this manifestation of evil," I said. "The criminally insane obsession with manufacturing and seeking out 'weapons of mass destruction' creates a scenario from hell, brought into your 'living room' in 'living' color and sound. Mass murder, torture, and dismemberment of Living creatures and all of the Elements is daily entertainment. The theme behind this made-for-TV war was Apocalypse Soon."

"Yes, and the invasion of Iraq was only one stage in Bush's attempt to manufacture a 'New World Order.' It fits together nicely with 'Homeland Security.' Dubya's brazen use of Nazi-sounding jargon gives the show away. It gives me chills," said Kate with a shudder.

"It feels to me as if the drum beats of the madmen's march toward Armageddon are sounding louder," I said. "Many women tell me that they are haunted by a sense of horror."

"And that is precisely why we invited you to visit us on Lost and Found Continent and why I am Here with you Now," Kate reminded me patiently. "It's Time for us to Realize our Temporal Convergence. We have gone before you, and we continue to go before you *with your help!* You are helping us Realize the Archaic Future, just as we are supporting you."

I gulped in astonishment at my own obtuseness. "How could I have these lapses into amnesia?" I muttered to no one in particular. Then, clearing my throat, I addressed my guest: "Thank you once again, Kate, for nudging me into Re-membering our empowering convergence," I said.

"Don't mention it," she responded. "Let's just contemplate the spectacle of the self-annihilation of patriarchy (which of course we

happily promote at every opportunity) and celebrate the Re-emergence of Biophilia."

"Sounds great to me!" I exclaimed. "Now, Kate, how about an
invigorating lunch break before we take our next Great Leap?"

Kate expressed her enthusiastic consent as we both stood up
and headed for the kitchen, where we searched in my well-stocked
refrigerator for some refreshing snacks.

CHAPTER TEN

SEEING THROUGH PHALLOCRACY'S BIGGEST LIES AND REVERSING ITS ROTTEN REVERSALS

WITH SOME HELPFUL PRODDING FROM KATE I took on the project of writing this chapter. I understood in a flash that what had been holding me back was paralysis at the thought of having to reinvent the wheel all over again. "Patriarchy has erected so many walls that block women from Seeing that they seem unable to overcome their fears," I muttered to mySelf.

"Stop muttering," I responded. "Just shut up and Go, and Leap, Mary, Leap!"

So that's when I decided to Fly again—no matter what! And I AM... throwing my life as far as it will go!

So what if they are lurching onward, destroying the environment? We could weep a thousand tears, crying endlessly. The point is to Live and Speak and Create Boldly, Regenerating Gynergy, which is not dead but Living Right Now, Right Here.

Just after I finished writing these words at about 4:00 a.m. the telephone rang. Feeling that this was a strange time for a phone call, I rather gingerly picked up the receiver. The voice on the other end was speaking in a foreign accent that I could not recognize. When I asked "Who is this?" the speaker seemed apologetic and hung up.

A few seconds later my fax machine signaled that a message was coming through. The fax was a beautifully written letter from a woman in Romania. The circumstances and the letter itself seemed to participate in an Other dimension, and it was in that Background dimension that the author of the letter (who wrote to me that her name is Ilinca) and I were connected and communicating.

In fact, we had been communicating for some Time, as Ilinca revealed in her descriptions of how she obtained my books and her reactions to them. In fact, there are many other examples of such Background communication, frequently involving my books. That means I *must* keep on writing.

At this point in my internal monologue, Kate, who had been sitting in Cottie's green chair, reading *1984*, interrupted my thoughts. "Isn't that because your books are Transtemporal mediums that carry messages through Time and Space?" she asked. "For those of us who have been reading them on Lost and Found Continent since the dawn of the Biophilic Era, the force that such books carry comes from the fact that they Challenge and Reverse and Jump beyond the foreground world of reversals which you and your comrades are always striving to transcend."

"The patriarchs have stolen the Power of Naming from women," I said. "They have replaced true words with verbal vomit. The phenomenon of reversal as the hallmark of phallocracy is illustrated in the absurd biblical story of Eve's birth and a million other lies. The early-twenty-first century's regurgitation of reversals and Biggest Lies is especially hideous. Maledom has come to its climax. The enormous volume of virile vomit fills the air and saturates the earth. Its sickening stench is omnipresent."

Kate sighed. "Of course, that's why my companions and I took off for Lost and Found. Oh, the aroma of pure air, of the sea, of grass! Thank Goddess for our escape!"

"I've been so Lucky to smell it, see it, breathe it, during my brief visits there. Thanks to all of you, Kate!" I said. "But I must continue my account of what is happening back here in the twenty-first century, archetypal deadtime."

Responding to my friend's nod of encouragement, I went on: "By the middle of the twentieth century it had already begun to be obvious to some people that extreme evil is widespread. The march of the Nazis to power in Germany, the holocaust of the Jews and other concentration camp inmates, including Gypsies, Slavs, prisoners of war, political prisoners, and homosexuals, the American atomic bombing of Hiroshima and Nagasaki in 1945—all were/are atrocities. But, of course, we can think back to the European witchburnings of the fifteenth, sixteenth, and seventeenth centuries and to worldwide atrocities before that. Atrocities have always been 'the usual' under patriarchy and legitimated by patriarchal scholarship."

"Yes indeed," sighed Kate. "So what do you experience as different about the early twenty-first century, Mary?"

"Of course, there is still more of the same, but there is also something else. Some clues about this can be found in the work of authors like John Pilger, who wrote in April 2003 that the unthinkable is becoming normalized.[1] The major means of legitimating, perpetuating, and escalating the horrors are the mainstream media, which normalize great crimes committed in our name by our government. The American-led 'wars' in Iraq have not been named as genocide, despite the blatancy of the fact that this was the agenda. Essayist Edward Herman wrote that following the 1991 Gulf War thousands of Iraqi teenage conscripts—many of them alive and trying to surrender—were buried by American bulldozers.[2] In December 1991 more than 200,000 Iraqi men, women, and children were killed or died as a result of the American-led attack on Iraq.[3]

"We know more now about the 1991 Gulf War and America's deliberate destruction of Iraq's civilian infrastructure. This destruction continued under G. W. Bush. As Pilger points out, by

July 2002 the United States was 'wilfully blocking humanitarian supplies worth 5.4 billion dollars, . . . all of which Iraq had paid for and the UN Security Council had approved.'[4] In the spring of 2003 the US and Britain attacked the sick and defenseless population of Iraq, which had no submarines, no navy, and no air force, and which was left without clean water, food, electricity, and anesthetics in its hospitals for the innumerable dismembered young victims of ruthless American military power."

Kate listened intently. "And this huge crime is called 'liberation'! The reversal is stunning."

"Yes," I agreed. "And Bush struts and proclaims 'victory.' It is important that we examine the meaning of the word *victory* now, in the present context."

SUMMONING OUR POWER TO OVERCOME THE "VICTORY" OF THE WARMONGERING REGIME

It was Memorial Day, and Kate had temporarily returned home to Lost and Found Continent and the Biophilic Era. She had said she needed some fresh air, inadvertently reminding me that I had almost forgotten what fresh air tastes and smells like. I was confident she'd be back soon.

Appropriately it was a dreary gray day, clouded with the unnatural overhanging smog of fear and despair, marked by a terrifying torrent of reversals that the media were blaring. I tried to remember that "memorial day" really means "forgetting day." I struggled not to forget what it was that I was supposed to remember, I mean, forget.

I was supposed to forget that women who are faithful to women and nature are rapidly being disappeared from prominence by the media and replaced by thoroughly assimilated women like Condoleezza Rice and Gale Norton, and numerous others. I was supposed to forget that I was trained to accept this situation and in fact be grateful for the tokens who were placed there in front of my eyeballs precisely so that I would not notice what is going on. I was supposed to remember that at least they are not wearing burqas. I was supposed to forget that I loathe their complicity. It goes on and on. I was beginning to feel exhausted by the process of reversing reversals, and especially by refuting and/or ignoring the women all around me who appear to have given up the struggle to remember not to forget.

In my mind's eye a group of women walked toward me, staring blankly. "Is this Stepford?" I frantically wondered out loud. Suddenly I heard familiar voices at the door. Hurrying across the room I met Kate and her daughter, Annie.

"I guess we're arriving just in Time!" exclaimed Kate.

"Yeah! We heard you raving," added Annie. "Don't worry, Mary. We're not the Stepford Wives coming to get you."

"Kate! Annie!" I yelled in relief. "Come in!"

Kate headed for her favorite chair. Annie, flopping down on the floor, exclaimed, "It's OK, we're here. Things must be getting worse and worse."

"You can say that again and again," I said. "But it's safe in here, as long as I keep the TV and radio off most of the time and, when necessary, screen my phone calls. Oh, yes, and I don't look too much at the newspapers. The disinformation can pop out and affect one when she least expects it."

"But hasn't that been the case for a long time already?" asked Annie.

I groped for the right words. "Yes, but there's now been an escalation almost to a point of critical mass of negativity, in the US especially. It was hard at first to let it all sink in. The Bush gang rigged the elections, bulldozed their way into control of all three branches of the US government, destroyed Iraq and its people (already broken down by Daddy Bush and the Gulf War and sanctions that meant starvation and desperate sickness). Now the bush gang swings their axes of evil, stationing swarms of american troops all over the world as they pursue their greed-propelled, criminally insane plans to build a giant empire and

acquire limitless corporate profit. Scary Junior Bush appears to
be a messianic madman, convinced that he is God's Chosen
One. His band of chickenhawks have plans for a Super War—
World War Four—which in fact has already been launched and
which will go on for many years, spreading to Iran, Egypt,
Saudi Arabia, the entire Middle East, and wherever else a government is in need of 'regime change.'"

While I caught my breath, my horrified guests sat and stared.

Before they could interrupt, I lurched on. "Add to all that the
bushite crimes against the planet itself. This is not just a footnote:
It goes to the core of the atrocities. As you know, whenever I speak
publicly I Invoke the Five Elements—the Earth, the Air, the Fire,
the Water, the Ether. When I do this, I am Be-Speaking into the
Ether—Naming patriarchy's rape of the Elements, which is the
primary and archetypal phallocratic mode of 'relating' to the environment. This has always been its way of dealing with Nature.
With the advent of modern technology, the horrors against the
environment have escalated immeasurably. We had become habit-
uated to gagging on contaminated air, choking on polluted water,
coughing on dust from the parched earth, and becoming blinded
by solar glare caused to a large degree by 'greenhouse gases' from
the american automobile industry. However, we glimpsed the
forthcoming extremities of environmental destruction from the
Bushes' 'precision' attacks on Iraq. For example, the large quanti-
ties of depleted uranium that have been left around are sources of
serious illness for many animals, including humans, for many
years to come."

"Mary, it's hard to think about this stuff all the time. Everyone
could be stopped dead by depression," said Kate.

"Yeah," agreed Annie. "Just one look at the faces of earth poi-
soners like dubya and his stooges—ignorant, arrogant, and uncar-
ing—is enough to knock me out."

"I agree wholeheartedly," I said. "Women must refuse to give
them our energy on any level. The need for women to reclaim our
Gynergy is urgent. But there seems to be a problem. Many

women apparently are seriously blocked when attempting to Re-Call Gynergy. We need to get past the blocks—sooner than soon—Now. But How?"

"I'm eager to know your answer to that question," said Annie. "So am I," I heartily agreed.

Demolishing the Blocks to Re-Calling Gynergy

While Annie helped herSelf to an apple from the bowl I had invitingly placed in front of her, I proceeded to develop the following response to my own hard question.

"You see, Annie," I began, "it's easy to recognize that women under patriarchy are blocked by fear—largely by media-manufactured fear—of poverty, of rejection, of isolation, of loneliness, of sickness. These dangers are real, of course, but I think it is necessary to raise the question Why are they apparently 'realer than real'? Why are they so overpowering/undermining that in recent years they have almost stopped our movement dead?"

I continued: "I suggest that the movement-stopping, consciousness-slopping power of this illusion/delusion stems from the fact that the phallocrats, neocons, heads of corporations, et cetera subliminally and overtly spread and repeat their message that 'things have always been like this,' or, more precisely, that 'patriarchy has always been around.' The implicit conclusion is 'You can never stop it; this is how things are.' When women buy this message, we die inside. Consciousness crumbles. We stumble around, stupefied."

As my Rage started to boil over, my voice grew louder. "This is the Biggest Lie of the 'neocons,' who are the same old cons. They con us by their smirks, their sneers. Their lies are literally written all over their faces/feces, their 'great books programs' in which the Truly Great Books of women, containing records of our very being, are erased, effaced.

"These are con artists," I yelled at my startled guests. "They are *the* essential essentialists. They wallow in the muck of reversals, calling women who dare to Re-Call our Archaic Powers 'essentialists.' They smirk at women who Name their games.

"We Curse the con men by be-ing our Selves. Be-Laughing Women laugh at our own Jokes, causing these fellows to shrivel into the nothingness which is their origin and their destiny."

Kate, who had been quietly sitting in the green chair, spoke up. "Their arrogant ignorance of everything before and beyond patriarchy is designed to silence women."

"Yes, Kate," I said. "But there is an abundance of evidence that they are wrong. World-renowned archeologist Marija Gimbutas and others have demonstrated this. As Joan Marler explains, Gimbutas' most striking research, which began in the late 1960s, showed that the earliest cultures were earth-based, peaceful, and highly developed, and not patriarchal and warlike as was commonly believed.[5] Marler points out:

> It was a radical retelling of the origins of Western civilization. The old idea was that civilization started with patriarchy—but that came later.[6]

"The disease called patriarchy is a blip on the screen of human history. It has been around for perhaps five thousand years and the Goddess culture has been here for many thousands of years."

Kate appeared relieved to hear this affirmation of the brevity of patriarchy's existence. "May that plague never return!" she exclaimed. "It has robbed Earth and her inhabitants of so much Life, Joy, and Hope. So long, phallocracy!"

"Right! Down with that perverted crap forever!" yelled Annie. Grabbing one of my pans and a large spoon, she banged on this improvised drum with glee. "May the Biophilic Era grow and expand all ways, always!" She and Kate, joined by my Lively Familiar, Cottie, Leaped around my apartment in a state of Ecstasy.

I stood up and called for a Moment of Silence. Then I read a statement written by Joan Marler in the late 1990s about the work of Marija Gimbutas. Marler stated:

Her work struck a chord that continues to resonate within and beyond academic spheres. It gives us a vision of what we can re-create. This view is giving us hope right at the end of the millennium, when most people envision apocalypse. There's a groundswell of people saying, "She's confirming what I know in my bones is true—we haven't always lived like this."[7]

I sat down and continued: "In a comparable sense Gimbutas also knew about this groundswell in her bones and was impelled to confirm it. Marler tells us:

Shortly after Marija Gimbutas died, I had a vivid dream that told me she is now in the realm of the ancestors. She spoke in a fierce voice, saying, 'You must remember us!' I was shaken awake with the distinct feeling that this dream was not only for me."[8]

I went on: "Not only in her books but also in interviews Marija gave many clues about what we must Re-member. For example, in one interview she described some features of Old European society which preceded patriarchal culture. She maintained that this pre-Indo-European, prepatriarchal society was matrifocal and matristic. Her choice of the word *matristic* rather than *matrifocal* is deliberate 'because *matriarchy* always arouses ideas of dominance and is compared with the patriarchy.'"[9]

"That word can be a real conversation stopper," commented Kate.

"Yes," I moaned. "The words are problematic. I prefer to say *gynocratic* or *gynocentric*, which are words that transcend fixation on motherhood, without excluding it."

"Right," responded Kate. "Certainly, many women choose not to be mothers. This fact should not be erased."

I continued: "Gimbutas insisted that Old European society was superior to what came later. She saw that it did not, and indeed could not, 'develop' into a patriarchal, warrior culture 'because this would be too sudden.' Its inhabitants had no weapons such as daggers or swords, just weapons for hunting. The invaders, who began coming from South Russia, had weapons and they had horses. As Gimbutas said: 'We have archaeological evidence that [there] was a *clash*. And then of course, who starts to dominate? The ones who have horses, who have weapons, who have small families and who are more mobile.'"[10]

Kate looked enraged. "And now, Mary, in your time, the military 'culture' spreads itself everywhere with its own vile 'weapons of mass destruction' that target all life on this planet, destroying nature itself. We on Lost and Found Continent are so glad that a re-emergence of Goddess consciousness is taking place in your time," she said. "This is of utmost importance, especially in the early twenty-first century."

"Marija Gimbutas was very optimistic about this," I said. "In her words:

> The Christian God punishes and is angry and does not fit into our times at all. We need something better. . . . We have to be grateful for what we have, for all the beauty, and the Goddess is exactly that. Goddess is nature itself. So I think this should be returned to humanity. I don't think that Christianity will continue for a very long time, but it's just like patriarchy, it's not easy to get rid of. But somehow, from the bottom up, it's coming.[11]

"I am interested in her straightforward comment 'Goddess is nature itself,'" I added. "So of course the malegod of patriarchy legitimates and requires the destruction of nature."

"Yes, nature is targeted by patriarchy, and especially by the patriarchal military profession," said Kate. "The Goddess-killers are by definition nature-killers. And as technological weaponry becomes ever more lethal the devastation of nature gets more widespread and irreversible."

"And the mindless destruction, which is fueled by hatred and utter lack of caring, parallels the phallocratic damage to women," I said. "I think that's a major reason why so many women intuitively can see the connections. We experience them in our lives. Rosalie Bertell, prolific scholar and activist in the field of environmental health, exemplifies this kind of astuteness in the realm of seeing links and noticing the failure of others to see them. In a 1993 article, 'Exposing the Agenda of the Military Establishment,' she wrote:

One very obvious omission at the Earth Summit in Rio de Janeiro was any discussion of the impact on the Earth's environment of war and preparation for war."[12]

I continued: "In that article Bertell moved on to an analysis of military involvement in environmental problems:

The major environmental problems—acid rain, ozone depletion, climate change, loss of topsoil, forest dieback, desertification and loss of tropical rainforests—all have military overtones. These combined ecopathologies have resulted in loss of species, increases in the rates of allergies, asthma, and cancer; and a greater number of congenitally damaged children. They have produced poverty, urbanization of farmers, and environmental refugees."[13]

I added: "And there's more."

"I'm sure!" groaned Kate. "It's already an overwhelming litany, and it's all I can digest for the moment."

Annie jumped in: "Aw Mom! I need to continue this conversation with Mary right now."

"That's fine. Go ahead!" replied her exhausted parent, as she curled up in her comfortable chair and dozed off.

"Well, good for Kate!" I commented. "Fire away, Annie!"

"I'd like to know if Rosalie Bertell moves beyond the terrible litany of ecopathologies," said Annie.

"Of course she does, Annie," I answered. "She points out that women, the so-called weaker sex, have highly developed special skills, particularly in the areas of cooperation and conflict resolution. You may be happy to learn that in her book *Planet Earth: The Latest Weapon of War*, Bertell offered no hope for the military. She took her stand as totally against war. Her critique of weaponry and warfare is devastating."

Kate joined in. "Yes, it's true. Such books are extremely important. But I'm feeling very impatient. I'm sure you can fill us in on the facts of Bush's vile war against women."

"Of course, Kate," I replied. "We know that he did his utmost—with the aid of Attorney General John Ashcroft and other woman-hating right-wing stooges—to reverse every victory gained by women in the twentieth century, such as the *Roe* decision and the Violence Against Women Act. VAWA gave new hope to hundreds of thousands of women in america who suffered from domestic violence in silent desperation. Look, here on my desk is a letter from the NOW Legal Defense and Education Fund, asking for money to support them in their fight for women's rights." I handed the letter to Annie.

Annie picked up the document and read aloud: "And his [Bush's] 'reforms' could turn deadly for the 60 percent of women on welfare who are victims of domestic violence, because he's earmarked more than one billion dollars for 'marriage promotion' programs that pressure women on welfare to marry, even if it means marrying a violent abuser."

"Yuk!" we yelled together.

At that Moment there was a polite tap on the door. We knew intuitively that this meant the arrival of a delegation from Lost and Found Continent.

"Come on in!" we all shouted, as Annie jumped up and opened the door. In rushed Anowa and Sophie, followed by Myoko, Nassrin, and Sung Hee. Without any need of formalities, they found space on the floor, as Annie helped me move around tables and other extraneous pieces of furniture to make room for them.

"Hey!" I exclaimed. "This is the first time we've all been together since my last visit to Lost and Found. What a wonderful surprise!"

My visitors began talking loudly all at once. I was about to ask them to cool it, when my Familiar, Cottie, came running in from her hiding place in my bedroom and jumped up on my desk, where she stood and stared imperiously. She was an awe-inspiring Presence.

We all understood the message Cottie was thinking to us. "Where are my friends, the Lost and Found Animals?"

Out loud, Annie asked: "Where are the animals from Lost and Found? Surely they could not have been forgotten? What happened?"

"Annie," I replied, "I seem to be getting the message from Cottie that they are, so to speak, on strike. They don't want to be 'brought along' by humans. They want their own significance and autonomy to be recognized." Cottie licked my arm as a token of encouragement. "OK," I stumbled on. "I believe they are letting us know that they want to be respected as their Selves."

"Yeah," said Myoko. "It's true that we all still have huge remnants of matronizing attitudes toward them. Even women on Lost and Found have memory lapses about the fact that it is the animals who are the Biophilic Cognitive Majority. Even though we are members of the necrophilic human species we are privileged to participate in that majority, and despite our frequent failures they put up with us."

"It must be difficult for them to be surrounded by such slow learners," commented Sophie. "I recall conversations from 'back then' when people referred to them as 'nonhuman animals.' I suppose the cats could refer to us as 'nonfeline animals' if they wished to sink to such a level of discourse. But they rarely show serious signs of impatience with our stupidity."

Sung Hee, who had become dreamy-eyed during this conversation, added, "It's about something bigger than just absence of impatience, though. Their patience with us comes from some deep and vast dimension of love. I was eavesdropping from Lost and Found when Mary described the experience she had when she was searching for Aille Og, who was 'the cat of *Quintessence*' and who disappeared shortly after that book was published. Mary and her friend June, who was searching with her in the small park on Crystal Lake where Aille Og had last been seen, experienced a powerful sense of unconditional love, which seemed to be coming from that wondrous cat as well as from the lake and far beyond. I was deeply moved by that description." Sung Hee looked at me for confirmation.

As I met Sung Hee's eyes, there was a gentle scratching at the door. "Oh, I wonder if that's a four-legged friend from Lost and Found. Maybe they have decided that we finally got the point," I said.

Everyone watched expectantly as Annie walked over and opened the door. We all were somewhat amused to see that our visitor was Annie's squirrel friend, popularly known as "Munchie." The squirrel hopped in boldly, glancing around expectantly. Since I was well aware of Munchie's habits, I hastened to pass her a dish of nuts from the coffee table.

We waited breathlessly while the new arrival sat up in the middle of the floor and enjoyed her snack. After she had munched her fill, she signaled Annie with her luxuriant tail. Annie, who had crept over to sit beside her, explained that her role was to translate for us the message that was being communicated telepathically by this small Ambassador from the animals of Lost and Found Continent. I can only summarize the gist of it here.

Munchie explained that she had been chosen for this mission for two reasons: First, there was her small size and agility. The animals had been told by Annie and Kate about the rather cramped space afforded by my apartment, which precluded the magnificent physical Presence of larger animals, like Annie's dear friend the Great Wolf Fenrir. Second, there was the fact of her close telepathic connection to Annie, which made possible precise communication and excluded forays into mere chattering, so to speak.

Munchie moved on to the substance of her message. She said that the Liberated Animals of Lost and Found—unlike those imprisoned by humans in archetypal deadtime/deadspace—had become more and more numerous and diverse and that adequate communication with them would require the sort of context provided by that Continent and by the Sense of Time/Timing signified by the expression *Biophilic Era*. She said that the main point to be considered here is the manifest reality of key patterns that connect diverse beings and manifestations of Be-ing. These, she asserted, are *Metapatterns*.[14]

Awed by the erudition and wisdom of the squirrel, we women were dumbstruck. My guests soon came to the conclusion that it was Time to go home to Lost and Found Continent and learn more from their animal friends in that context. They entreated Cottie and me to visit them there as soon as possible.

We gratefully accepted this invitation and promised to come very soon.

Chapter Eleven

The Animals—Here and There

Back at ground zero in archetypal deadtime, I performed some necessary tasks, such as grocery shopping, while often daydreaming about upcoming Transtemporal Travels. After one prosaic shopping trip, as I was schlepping bags of groceries from my car and up the stairs to my apartment, on my way up I was greeted with Wild enthusiasm by the friendly Irish setter who lives downstairs. I, of course, responded with matching enthusiasm.

As I unpacked the bags on the kitchen table I kept thinking about dogs and cats. Cottie, who had greeted me with sweet feline affection at the door of our apartment, seemed to be reading my mind. No doubt she sensed my preoccupation.

When I walked into the living room and sat down on the couch with my coffee, she jumped onto her green chair, which was situated directly across from me, and lay down with an air of deliberation and proprietorship. This seemed like an elaborate performance, conveying the message "I am your Familiar, working with you in the process of creating *Amazon Grace*." She was also portending something Momentous that was about to happen.

As on previous occasions, Cottie sat up and faced the bookcase beside her chair, leaned with her forepaws on its arm, and then picked out a book with one of her paws. This was *The Greek Myths* by Robert Graves, in which he wrote:

> The transition . . . to patriarchy seems to have come about in Mesopotamia, as elsewhere, through the revolt of the Queen's consort to whom she had deputed executive power by allowing him to adopt her name, robes, and sacred instruments.[1]

The primary significance of this passage to me was the mention of Mesopotamia as a locus of "transition" from matriarchy (*sic*) to patriarchy. Among the vilest effects of G. W. Bush's criminal war against Iraq (formerly Mesopotamia) was the destruction of archeological sites. Some of these probably included important clues about gynocratic society in prepatriarchal times.

The most inspiring "find" of Cottie, however, was not Graves' book, but a very different volume. After she searched further, my Feline Familiar Archeologist picked out another book very deliberately and obviously. I walked over and pulled it out easily. Carrying it over to my desk, I saw that it was *Mind and Nature: A Necessary Unity*, by Gregory Bateson.[2]

Glancing through a few introductory pages which I had underlined some twenty years previously, I noticed Bateson's preoccupation with the phrase "the pattern which connects." Pondering this phrase, he states:

> My central thesis can now be approached in words: The pattern which connects is a metapattern. It is a pattern of patterns. It is that metapattern which defines the vast generalization that, indeed, it is patterns which connect.[3]

Bateson also offers the reader the notion of context, of pattern through time. These phrases triggered my memories of my own thoughts about *Metapatterning*.

The reader may ask: "But where does he go with this?" My blunt response is: To somewhere in his own context. But that doesn't matter to me at this point. I have come to learn from these adventures with Cottie that my job is to absorb the memory jolt but not become distracted from my own purpose by wandering off into the thought processes of any particular author, such as Bateson, whose metapattern is not Metapatriarchal.

In this instance Cottie was nudging me into refocusing on my own path of Dis-covering Lost and Found Continent and its animal inhabitants by reminding me of my own word, *Metapatterning*. This word was first explained at some length in *Pure Lust*.[4] It was later defined in the *Wickedary* as the

> process of breaking through paternal patterns of thinking, speaking, acting; Weaving the way through and out of male-ordered mazes; Metapatriarchal Erratic Movement.[5]

And this is what the animals and women of Lost and Found Continent are doing. It is what they are about. Animals and women become Untamed, Undisconnected.

When I am Metapatterning Here at home, naturally I am moving toward and with those animals and women. Cottie is Dis-covering her identity as a Lost and Found Cat. We are Present in a Transtemporal cosmic dance together.

Experiences of interspecies communication are not uncommon, although many persons who had such encounters in childhood may have forgotten them because of bombardments of nonconsciousness in the dulled-out climate of the foreground.

An outstanding example of a woman who has not forgotten is Kay Mann, an interspecies communicator who Re-members and who uses her Gift to help hundreds of animals and people who call upon her for help. In a conversation with Kay she explained to me that as a child—and throughout her adult life—she was really hearing what animals were thinking. Kay also knew if an animal was ill. She recalls making comments such as "That dog is pale," and then explaining to the surprised listener, "I see things differently than you do." Kay also told me that she spent more time with animals than with other children. This struck me as an excellent choice.

Kay Mann helped me with emergencies that affected all three of my Feline Familiars who were Present for the writing of my books. In the course of our conversations she explained that these animals were "enlightened beings" entrusted to my care. Such animals are "Master Teachers," and we are their "caretakers." They exude "pure love, gentleness, and patience."

This information has been confirmed by my own experiences over time. As it has deepened and expanded I have come to realize that the greatest block to this evolution of awareness is my own susceptibility to distraction by inane, pseudo-important, and sometimes academented "issues." The one who can bring me back into Focus, of course, is my Familiar. *Familiar* is defined in the *Wickedary* as "a Super Natural Spirited Background Animal, the Graceful Friend of a Witch."[6]

According to Wiccen tradition, Familiars are of two kinds: Domestic Familiars and Divining Familiars. My readers are aware of the fact that at Present my Domestic Familiar is a Stunning Feline Named Cottie. *Cot*, of course, means "cat" in Gaelic. Cottie's mother is a barn cat who lived and worked in a town in Maine; I suspect that Cottie's ancestry goes back to Ireland since her wittiness/Sparkiness has a certain quality which my admittedly prejudiced perceptions tend to identify as Irish. At any rate, together we have Sparked ideas for this book.

According to the great author of *The Witch-Cult in Western Europe*, Margaret A. Murray, Divining Familiars do not belong to the Witch but appear accidentally after the performance of certain magical ceremonies.[7] The phrase "magical ceremonies" can be interpreted in various ways. The point is that "stuff happens," and then these truly magical animals appear. The following account illustrates the manifestation of an animal whom I would identify as a Divining Familiar.

THE STORY OF A COW NAMED EMILY

Hundreds, perhaps thousands, of persons met one particularly
Magical Animal who charged into fame on November 15, 1995,
after charging out of a slaughterhouse in Hopkinton, Massachu-
setts, just Moments before she would have been murdered. She
was a Cow who came to be known as Emily.

Emily's celebrated escape from a Hopkinton holding pen was
accomplished by jumping over a five-foot fence. This feat was followed by several weeks of wandering through snow-covered
woods. She was aided by an "underground railroad" of animal
lovers who helped her to elude capture for forty days, after which
the Sherborn Peace Abbey negotiated a deal to buy her for one
dollar. Described as "the poster child for vegetarianism" by an in-
tern, Emily the Cow was more than this. She had the gift of being
simply Present.

Emily had her own special barn, with a playmate—a young
steer named Gabriel. They had a beautiful field in which they
could run, play, and graze. It was a blissful space and time. Emily's
courage, charm, intelligence, and grace were there to be experienced by the one hundred or so visitors who came to see her every
week. I was Lucky enough to be one of these guests, and I even
had a private audience with the Bovine Wonder. I could see that
the Spark in her eyes cut through all pretense.

Emily died prematurely of uterine cancer in March 2003 at the
age of ten. She was buried behind the Gandhi statue at the Peace
Abbey on April 2.

Although Emily's life was cut short, her work is not done. As
Kathy Berghorn wrote:

> There can be no "final respects" to you, Emily, and there can be no
> closure until the last slaughterhouse has closed its doors, until all
> beings show compassion to each other, locally and globally. This is
> a process that will outlive me, too. Your courageous life journey will
> be an ongoing reminder that I must never give up. You never did.[8]

Emily the Cow is indeed a great teacher, inspiring those who know and love her to jump over the fence of the slaughterhouse in which we have languished far too long. To me she is an Ambassador from the Dimension of Lost and Found, inviting her friends to summon Courage to escape from archetypal deadtime and Realize Life in the Biophilic Era. We will find her there!

As Kay Mann pointed out: "There's a groundswell now of individuals who realize that animals are important." This says it succinctly. And the powerful response to Emily the Cow is evidence of this groundswell.

The torture and destruction of animals throughout patriarchal history is a true horror story which is mind-boggling. Few persons are capable of grasping its scope and the hideous details of the acts of cruelty and wanton greed which it has entailed. Even fewer seem to be capable of retaining this information and behaving ethically and consistently in response to knowledge of unconscionable behavior. Most remain frozen in denial, placidly eating their roast beef dinners and less expensive carnivorous fare like Big Macs, for example. Yet, for as long as we allow these atrocities to continue without protest, human beings have no right to live on Earth.

In contrast to the unspeakable cruelty of humans to Other animals, the latter continue to bestow on members of this arrogant and frequently vicious species their Divine, Unconditional Love.

In the face of such contradictions, as they become ever more evident, we grope for words or perhaps just turn aside. Yet everywhere we see evidence of destruction of life on Earth.

Immersed in these thoughts, I cried out: "Where is Biophilia?"

As if on cue, there was a polite but insistent knocking on the door. Without waiting for me to get up and open it, Anowa, Annie, and Fenrir strode in.

"You know Where/When it is," Anowa yelled at me. "Come on along with us!"

Fenrir comfortingly put her paw on my arm, while Annie dragged down my suitcase from the closet, pulled out some of my clothes, and hastily began to pack them. "It's a good thing you did your laundry recently," she muttered.

Seeing what was going on, Cottie jumped into my suitcase, where she appeared to be trying on my pajamas. "No time for these tricks now, Cottie," I told her, while I snatched her into my arms. "Oh, will you toss in a few bags of cat treats, Annie?" I shouted, as Fenrir happily led the way out the door.

"Ready, set, go!" yelled Annie.

"No need for explanations. There'll be plenty of Time for discussion on Lost and Found Continent," Anowa added.

"You always have a two-way ticket!" shouted Annie.

"Yeah, I've used them before," I replied.

CHAPTER TWELVE

IN THE LIGHT OF THE BRONTOSAURUS

WHEN WE ARRIVED AT OUR DESTINATION we were greeted by throngs of Lost and Found animals. Among these appeared a beautiful dinosaur. Cottie was astonished at her first glimpse of such a creature. She appeared to be unafraid, however. Indeed, she stepped right over to a huge lizard-footed individual, about sixty feet long, whom she seemed to recognize as herbivorous, and fearlessly sniffed her toes.

"Cottie!" I yelled in alarm. Anowa nudged my arm and whispered, "Don't worry, it's just a brontosaurus looking for some delicious vegetarian food."

Choking back my terror, I pleaded, "Please help me rescue my cat!"

"There's no need to be afraid, Mary," responded Anowa. "Come on!" We ran over together to the dinosaur and cat. I snatched my Familiar and fled from the apparently oblivious brontosaurus. After we rushed back to the spot where we had originally been standing and watching, I struggled to catch my breath.

"Hey, what's going on, anyway?" I asked. "I thought we were just going for a pleasant walk Here after that astonishingly fast trip from my apartment, and I suddenly realized that we'd come upon a dinosaur! Lost and Found Continent appears to have changed quite a bit!"

As we sat down on the grass I gazed around at the various animals, who were politely ignoring us while they went about their own business. I suspected that they were giving me a chance to adapt to the new situation.

"Well," commented Anowa, "you recall that you and many others in the twenty-first century a.d. were concerned about the disappearing of species. You see, in the past few years we on Lost and Found have been approached by many animals seeking a home here. As it happens, the animal population has increased. Many who were believed to have become extinct managed to find their way here. This is, after all, the Biophilic Era. Naturally, Life thrives Here."

"Do you think that brontosaurus is thriving?" I asked rather contentiously. "And as a matter of fact I notice that there are quite a few small animals in the crowd nearby. It makes me nervous to see that. Aren't you concerned that some of them might be accidentally—uh—crushed?"

"It's interesting that you bring that up," replied Anowa. "In fact, a number of us held a meeting earlier this afternoon about the issue of the brontosaurus. (We already have a nickname for her—'Brontie.') Some of us were worried about the possibility Brontie might not be able to consider adequately the consequences of her behavior and, well, step on someone."

"That's an important consideration," I said.

Anowa looked relieved to see that I understood. "You see, Mary, it all happened very fast. First, Brontie sent us a telepathogram, asking us whether she could come to Lost and Found for a visit. Since none of us had ever met a dinosaur, and since the tone of her message conveyed that she had a very unassuming personality, we felt a strong empathy for her. Also, as you and Sophie and Kate have told us 'kids,' some women have even been called 'dinosaurs' back there/then when they 'stuck to their

guns' so to speak, and refused to give in to the newest academented fads, like postmodernism and postfeminism. So we did
invite her to come over Here for a vacation."

"And has it been a good experience?" I asked.

"Yes, absolutely," replied Anowa. "She is a gentle and delightful
being and regales us with stories about the Mesozoic Era. That's
why we sort of closed our eyes to the possibility of any danger in
the situation. We wouldn't want to hurt her feelings for anything."

I saw that Anowa felt conflicted and distressed. "But you only
invited her to come for a vacation, and that was all she asked for,"
I reminded her. "Maybe she is satisfied with her visit and will be
happy to return to When she came from."

Again I saw that Anowa looked relieved. "I'll have to talk it
over with Annie and Sophie and Kate before speaking with Brontie," said Anowa.

"Good idea," I said. "I suggest that when you do speak with
Brontie you be completely honest with her. I have a hunch that
she will understand."

I was eager to visit with these good friends, but I realized that
I was too tired to chat for very long after such an eventful day.
Annie and Kate had a room ready for me and I "crashed out" al-
most immediately.

When I woke up it was the next morning and the smell of coffee was inviting. Annie and Kate brought me breakfast in bed.
"Wow!" I said. "All the comforts of home!"

"We know your accustomed lifestyle!" said Kate. Everyone
laughed.

Suddenly Anowa came rushing in. "Mary, you'll never guess
who came to visit me last evening!"

"But let me try to guess anyway," I said. "Was it Brontie?"

"Yes!" exclaimed Anowa. "First I heard loud footsteps and the
sound of crashing branches. I didn't have to wonder who was approaching! I looked out the door and saw Brontie's enormous
form coming toward me. Since she obviously could not fit into my
house, I met her outside on the lawn. Brontie came right to the

point. She told me that she had a wonderful Time on Lost and
Found, but that she felt drawn to go back to When she came
from. I agreed, but I prevailed upon her to stay for part of the next
day, at least. (That's today!) I explained to her that it was important for us to have a discussion with her about species that have
disappeared, are disappearing, or will disappear back there/then. I
added with enthusiasm that she would be 'the Life of the party' at
such a discussion and that we would love to prolong her visit because we'll miss her, Naturally/Super Naturally. So our meeting
was set for two o'clock this afternoon on Lost and Found Beach."

There was a sense of excitement swirling around us. It was
coming not only from the Gynergetic interactions among the five
of us but from the Biophilic atmosphere of Lost and Found. I
could hear the enthusiasm in the voices and movements of animals who were not far away—their chirps, squeals, barks, moos,
howls, whines, whistles, hoots. Everyone was connecting with
everyone else. The trees were waving their arms in rhythm with
the sounds of voices and movements of all of us. To put it another
way, "everyone" was sounding and moving in harmony with the
breathing and arm-waving of the trees.

Together we women Re-Called our Momentous meeting that
took place on Lost and Found Beach in 2048 BE. We spoke of
how we had raged and sobbed at the thought of the arrogance and
stupidity of those men who tortured and destroyed the Earth's
creatures, claiming as justification their deceptive belief that "animals don't suffer." Myoko had loudly bemoaned the fact that they
had "created" monstrously deformed creatures by genetic manipulation—invading their genetic core. But even more significant was
the ultimate Sense of harmony and bonding among the plants, animals, and women and the participation of all in the dance of synchronicity in the universe.

I stated emphatically that I wanted to thank Annie for her
splendid description of that earlier Moment, which was published
at the end of *Quintessence* in her "Cosmic Comments and Conversations in 2048 BE Concerning Chapter Five."

Annie smiled and stood up (predictably) to take a bow. We all applauded loudly. Then we suddenly realized that it was Time to head for our Second Great Gathering on Lost and Found Beach.

We arrived quite early, and as we approached the beach we saw a gigantic solitary being sitting on the sand, gazing out at the sky. We recognized Brontie, and as we came closer we saw that she was apparently in such a state of Rapture that she didn't even hear us approaching. And she looked . . . Beautiful!

Quietly we all sat on the ground before her. We somehow understood that she was intending to communicate to us Archaic Wisdom from her own Time, the Mesozoic Era, approximately 160 million years ago.

The communication, of course, was beyond words. Sophie told me later that she had experienced something like a quality of Light that enhanced her intellect so that she Saw *through* "normal" perceptions. It was, she said, like seeing and feeling an extraordinarily beautiful sunset—expanding and intensifying. She added that it was be-ing in Harmony with Reality, or be-ing in Touch with Be-ing.

We all more or less agreed with this description of the effect of Brontie's Presence. Speaking for myself, I said that I was deeply ashamed of my earlier reactions to Brontie, especially my underestimation of her intelligence and sensitivity. Anowa said she felt the same way. So did everyone else.

"So much of our 'education' is glorified arrogant ignorance," I said in disgust. "Cottie had it right when she ran straight over to Brontie. And of course she would not have been stepped on by this remarkable being!"

"This is a precious Moment," remarked Kate. "While we are in the Presence of this Light, it is important to clarify our thoughts about 'extinct species.' It seems to me that we should distinguish between extinctions that occurred millions of years ago and extinctions that are happening in this century and are attributable to human behavior."

"I agree with that, Kate," I said. "It would not be reasonable to think that the extinction of the dinosaurs was caused by humans, but humans now are directly responsible for the disappearing of species in large numbers. An article in *The New York Times* by James Gorman contains important information on this subject:

> An international group of 19 scientists, analyzing research around the globe, has concluded that a warming climate will rival habitat destruction in prompting widespread extinctions in this century.[1]

"The article goes on to say that according to these scientists, if warming trends continue, 15 to 37 percent of the 1,103 species they studied will be doomed."

"Oh, it's their usual vague gobbledygook," Anowa moaned.

"Yes," I said. "The researchers were described as 'surprised' and 'shocked' by their findings. Many of us have been thinking and saying similar things for some time, but the researchers have the numbers and professional standing, and that gives them credibility—even though they admit that there's a huge amount of uncertainty. They also asserted that they did not predict that all the extinctions will have occurred by 2050, but that by that time the species under their consideration will have reached a point of no return.

"I suspect that their uncertainty is primarily about specific dates, numbers, and names of species that will become extinct, and exactly where they are to be found," I added. "In their study they included species in different terrestrial environments around the world—Europe, Central America, South America, Australia, and Africa."

"Of course, many people will immerse themselves in the usual foreground distractions to reinforce the state of denial," remarked Sophie. "You, Mary, can set an example by your travels into the Biophilic Era. These are manifestations of the 'Qualitative Leaping' you've been talking and writing about for many years and which you've subsequently often called 'quantum leaping,' evoking the context of the 'new physics.' We especially love the fact that you created the expression 'Lusty Leaping.'[2] Whatever the significance of the nuances implied in the various expressions, there is one common element: Hope, which you sometimes call 'Hopping Hope' in *Pure Lust* and in the *Wickedary*."

"Yeah, Sophie," I said, "the *Wickedary* defines this as 'Hope that hops, leaps, jumps intuitively in harmony with the rhythms of the Elemental world.'"[3]

"I love to talk about Hopping Hope," I added. "It makes me think of rabbits and kangaroos, oh!—and birds! It makes me happy just to think about it!"

"You waxed eloquent about it in *Pure Lust*," Sophie exclaimed, waving a tattered copy of that book. "I just happen to have a copy of that book with me," she added with a smile. "Here it is." Flipping through the pages, she commented: "You link it up with the behavior of 'Fey Women.' Remember what you wrote in Chapter Eight:

> A Fey woman/Hag can hope because she can hop, leap, jump intuitively. To put it another way, her cognitive and affective rhythms are not tidy. They are Tidal, responding to her Elemental context.[4]

"And a little further on there is a passage about 'mythic giant steps past the foreground':

> The Movements that "count" are Metaphoric Springs of consciousness, and of behavior consistent with this consciousness.[5]

"And yet a bit further on:

> As Fates, Fey women bound and bond biophilically with each other, and with the sun and the moon, the tides, and all of the elements. Our Time is relative to this ever moving context."[6]

I tried to maintain my composure. In the face of such flattering attention to my written words I was really quite embarrassed. However, I managed to say, "Well, you Foresisters of the Future seem to understand my work. And you, Sophie, really get the point about Hopping Hope in *Pure Lust!*"

To my astonishment, my remarks were met with gales of laughter.

When this subsided, Sophie, who was wiping tears from her eyes, replied in a booming voice: "WELL, YOU'D BETTER BELIEVE THAT WE UNDERSTAND YOUR WORK AND THAT I 'GET THE POINT' ABOUT HOPPING HOPE." Then she asked in a soft tone that was almost a whisper: "*Who do you think was helping you write your books?*"

There was a brief period of silence while the import of Sophie's words "sank in." I simply said, "Oh, of course! You Future Foresisters on Lost and Found have been inspiring and helping me right along!"

"And we are always working together," Sophie added. "The response of Biophilic women to the ultimate horror that is being perpetrated by patriarchy—the extinction of living creatures on this planet—is Hopping Hope, which implies Leaping, Elemental consciousness and behavior. It is the response we must make to the despair that is at the core of patriarchal necrophilia," she concluded, quietly and fiercely.

Then I began to Laugh Out Loud. The animals—who were Be-Laughing in their own variety of styles—and the other women on Lost and Found Beach joined in. Our Be-Laughing became louder and Louder and rippled out over the sea as more and more Lost and Found animals and women approached the Beach.

Suddenly, Cottie, who had been following us at a distance, broke through the crowd and ran over and joined our group—perhaps I should say "class"—and sat at the feet of Brontie, whose mystical multicolored Light was expanding and enveloping us. As this light shifted, so did our awareness. We knew that we were being called upon to Conquer the apparently unconquerable, the necrophilic biocidal mania of archetypal deadtime. Once again, Re-Calling our first Celebration together on Lost and Found Beach in 2048 BE, the multitude of women Here and Now stood and joined in the Biophilic telepathic chorus of the animals: "*We have overcome!*"

Chapter Thirteen

Facing the Current Mass Extinction: Rising to the Challenge of Re-Claiming Biophilia

When I returned from my latest trip to the Biophilic Era I was filled with excitement and expectation. I felt a shift in the morphic field. It was Time for me to wake up and Fiercely Face the damage that was being caused by the omnicidal maniacs in the early twenty-first century of archetypal deadtime.

I hurried to my computer and opened to the main website that I could find on the current mass extinction. This appeared under the title "Mass Extinction Underway." I was immediately faced with announcements such as the following:

> Human beings are currently causing the greatest mass extinction of species since the extinction of the dinosaurs 65 million years ago. If present trends continue one half of all species of life on earth will be extinct in 100 years.[1]

And it may be sooner than that. The website contains hundreds of links to horrifying authoritative reports that have become available within the past few years and informs its readers that new articles are added regularly. We are given a foretaste of information contained in the listed links, for example:

A new global study concludes that 90 percent of all large fishes have disappeared from the world's oceans in the past half century.[2]

And again:

Lion populations have fallen by almost 90 percent in the past 20 years, leaving the animal close to extinction in Africa. . . . There are now only 23,000 left, compared to an estimated 200,000 two decades ago.[3]

This material is presented together with an article by Joby Warrick that appeared in *The Washington Post*, maintaining that "a majority of the nation's biologists are convinced that a 'mass extinction' of plants and animals is underway that poses a major threat to humans in the next century."[4]

The impact of this poll of scientists was heightened by more recent research, such as I mentioned in Chapter 12, whose results were announced in January 2004.[5] In that year the first comprehensive study into the effect of higher temperatures on the natural world was completed. The sheer scale of the disaster facing the planet shocked those involved in the research, who estimated that more than one million species will be lost by 2050. It had finally become clear that climate change is the greatest single threat to survival of species.

Since there is a continuing outpouring of new knowledge, it is important to keep in touch with the most recent developments. It is essential, however, not to stop at collecting bits of information. In order to provide a context, some focus on theoretical and historical work is necessary. Particularly useful is the book *The Sixth Extinction* by world famous paleoanthropologist Richard Leakey and his colleague Roger Lewin.[6]

Leakey and Lewin explain that our planet has been shaken by five major extinctions in the four-billion-year history of life. The first occurred 450 million years ago. The fifth mass extinction, caused by Earth's collision with an asteroid, happened 65 million years ago, at the end of the Cretaceous period, and ended reptilian domination of our planet. This was the age of the extinction of the dinosaurs, and it led to the current mammalian domination of Earth.[7]

Leakey maintains that the Sixth Extinction is the next annihilation of vast numbers of species, which is happening *now*. *Homo sapiens* is responsible for this overwhelming mass extinction, which threatens the entire web of life on earth.[8]

This would seem to be the worst of news. Yet Leakey himself focused a positive spotlight on the problem. He wrote the following lines on the last page of his book:

> For a long time mass extinctions were a neglected subject of study, because they were mysterious in many ways and, anyway, were thought to be mere interruptions in the flow of life. They are now recognized as a major creative force in shaping that flow, and they will surely continue to be so for billions of years into the future, long after *Homo sapiens* and its descendants are no more.[9]

If Leakey is offering hope, it must be rooted at least partially in the idea that mass extinctions are "a major creative force in shaping" the flow of life and will continue to be. These words seem to be consistent with the widespread recognition that dissipation of form may make way for the emergence of new forms, more suitable to the newly prevailing conditions.

Leakey frequently uses the expression "accident of history" to describe the human species. He is fully aware that such language will be met with resistance by those who feel threatened by it.

Of course, if the reader's imagination is dominated by a picture of a "divine being," a noun-god with a blueprint in his imaginary hand for his imaginary creatures, such language may be experienced as shocking. Insofar as she is liberated from such images, language such as that of Leakey will be experienced as less and less threatening. It will not function as a serious stumbling block to her own Sense that there is purpose in Be-ing, in which we all participate. Nor will it blunt her intuitive understanding that Hopping Hope is alive and working well as a mode of Moving On.

Hopping/Hoping On

Earlier in this book I have written about the principal ways by which human beings have acted to destroy the inhabitants of Earth, including ourselves. United Nations demographers estimate that world population—now fast approaching seven billion—will increase 45 percent by 2050. The United Nations Environment Program (UNEP) also claims that the natural environment will be increasingly stressed if present trends in population growth, economic growth, *and consumption patterns* continue. This is not hard to illustrate. Take the following example of a consumption pattern in action.

Anyone who has driven in a city such as Boston and the surrounding area in the first decade of the twenty-first century with eyes and ears open must sense the increasing stress on everything and everyone, including herself. She will, of course, notice the mass of evidence that people driving while using cell phones, during the rush hours especially, are microwaving their brains out—unless she is using a cell phone herself. If she is still Conscious, there is hope that she will Sense an invisible electrosmog engulfing her.

Insofar as her awareness manages to expand further, she may be shocked into glimpsing the fact that this smog itself is expanding to join all other comparable man-made radioactive microcosms that are engulfing the entire planet.

Let's optimistically assume that our Boston driver has by now switched off her cell phone and pulled over to the side of the road in order to think more clearly. She might contemplate the situation as follows: The man-made electromagnetic field of physical and mental pollution, as it expands, is choking off life—her life and all life on Earth.

If she is Lucky, however, she will also Re-Call that there are other kinds of fields. For example, as we have seen earlier in this book, there are morphogenetic fields—morphic fields which play a causal role in morphogenesis. These nonmaterial regions of influence allow for the emergence of New Forms. They are Biophilic Fields. Even in times of decay and dissipation, they are Life-engendering, as opposed to merely death-dealing.

Before Spiraling back and onward to a further consideration of these Biophilic fields, I will make a brief detour to an article in the June 2004 issue of *The Ecologist*.[10] The title of the article as well as the issue—"Killing Fields"—refers primarily to destructive electromagnetic fields. This title is evocative, a stroke of genius perhaps, because it attracts interest and because it sparks off a multiplicity of meanings and associations.

I was struck by the presence of the word *fields* in this title.[11] The word itself suggests to me positive "magnetic fields" and "morphogenetic" fields. It shimmers with energy and power of attraction. However, when it is combined with the word *killing*, it re-sounds with an electrifying crash. One can hear *killing* as adjectival, suggesting "fields that kill." This is accurate and powerful, when applied to man-made electromagnetic fields. But of course the reader can also hear *killing* as a verb whose object is *fields*. This interpretation is enormously suggestive. It raises the question: Who (or what) is killing what?

Clearly, high-voltage power lines and mobile phone masts are constantly operational sources of man-made electromagnetic radiation (EMR), which they emit ceaselessly, creating a field of low-frequency radiation.[12] Many people and other animals live within or close to such hazardous areas and are the victims of such killing fields. There are also countless household sources— anything electrical—which expose us to short doses of EMR. We are well advised to use such products as briefly as possible and keep our distance from them. Maintaining a distance of two feet minimizes exposure, we are told. I do not find this information to be consoling. The problems are too complex and vast for band-aid (and/or measuring tape) solutions.

The scope of the human predicament at this point in history is enormous. The problem is discussed in *Quintessence*, specifically in "Cosmic Comments and Conversations in 2048 BE Concerning Chapter Two":

> Our planet is protected from the full force of the sun's energy by its geomagnetic field. Without this field life could not exist. But there have been changes underneath this "umbrella."[13]

The passage continues with a quote from Robert O. Becker, who wrote in the 1990s that "since humanity has learned how to generate and manipulate electromagnetic forces, we have created other forces beneath this shield, the likes of which have never before existed."[14] He pointed out that "we swim in a sea of energy that is almost totally man-made" and referred to this environment as "the electromagnetic jungle that now surrounds us."[15]

In this section of *Quintessence*, I had just arrived on Lost and Found Continent during one of my Time-Traveling visits to the Archaic Future. It is 2048 BE, and I am listening to Annie, who is describing some problems she and other inhabitants of Lost and Found are having. Annie mentions "surges of hostility" and "unexpected lapses into mean-spirited behavior." She says that even those who were born on Lost and Found appear to have slipped into what I and my contemporaries describe as "ingrained bad habits." She adds: "We've all been shocked and stunned by this regression."[16]

The paragraphs that follow these remarks contain my responses to and reflections on Annie's descriptions of the problems of women in 2048 BE. I suggest that it makes sense that the inhabitants of Lost and Found are still suffering from toxic residues of the patriarchal system. I also state that just as the Earth is still cleansing herSelf of toxins from the terrible patriarchal time, Annie and her contemporaries have to keep on expelling the emotional poisons that are still around.

Reflecting upon the possibility that there are connections between the Elemental Magnetism of Earth's inhabitants and the condition of Earth's magnetic field, I made the following observation: "In the 1990s researchers working with a variety of techniques came to the conclusion that a 'quiet' geomagnetic field enhanced... [the capacity for what] they inaccurately called 'extrasensory perception'—and which I have called Elemental Sensory Perception—while a disturbed geomagnetic field interferes with such powers. ESP as we experience it is essential to the workings of our Magnetic powers. The Earth's magnetic field was seriously disturbed at that time [and on into the twenty-first century] by the proliferation of man-made electromagnetic fields, especially those generated by the military establishment."[17]

Shortly after this analysis, *Quintessence* continues with a description of the fragmented condition of women in archetypal deadtime. Again, it is Mary (i.e., myself) whom we hear/overhear as she depicts for Annie in 2048 BE just how things were "back then":

> There was fragmentation everywhere in society, and it was especially devastating among women.... The breaking off of friendships, the abandonments and betrayals were so flagrant and common that many were disheartened and simply withdrew their energies from the cause of women. All of us sometimes felt baffled and confused. The comment that I heard most commonly was "I just don't understand what is happening!" Wild Women were aware of the Magnetic field of force that could still be Conjured among us. But....[18]

At this point I found myself unable to continue reading the passage from *Quintessence,* because I was stunned by an odd but

familiar interruption. First, I Sensed a shift in the fields. Then I
was shocked by the sound of Annie's voice yelling: "*Please stop
reading, Mary!*" So I stopped in mid-sentence and gaped in surprise when I saw Annie herSelf right in front of me.

"Well, you really don't pull your punches, do you, Annie?" I
commented, as we greeted each other affectionately. "I suppose
that my reading from your 'Cosmic Comments and Conversations
in 2048 BE Concerning Chapter Two' sort of worked as a way of
Invoking you, although I was not fully conscious that this was
happening. But why did you yell at me to stop reading from the
book at that point?"

"Because I knew what was coming next in the text, and this is
very hard stuff, as you know."

"Oh, come on, Annie," I groaned. "Since when have you shied
away from 'hard stuff'?"

At this point Cottie came bounding into the room, jumping
and leaping all over the furniture. First she hopped onto my desk.
Next she pounced onto the table holding *The American Heritage
Dictionary* and began flipping the pages. Without letting me
know what she was hunting for, she then dashed into the kitchen
and back again, hurling herself onto the couch, where she lay,
Wild-eyed and panting. After a few minutes she sat up and stared
at us with apparent disdain, as if to say, "Well, don't you get it? I'm
doing my best to communicate with you!"

Annie and I were just standing there gaping, and no doubt
looking quite stupid.

Then Annie turned to me and began speaking slowly. "I think
she's trying to convey something, Mary," she said. "I can feel her
pulling information from my brain."

"Well, good for you both!" I snapped. "Don't think I feel left
out or anything like that!" I glared at Cottie. "My very own Familiar!" I moaned accusingly at the cat, who simply gave me a big
wink.

Annie and I both burst out laughing, while my Feline companion stalked over and rubbed her head on my arm.

"OK," I said. "We all know that cats are experts in the field of Jealousy. Well, Annie, please clue me in. What information do you think this one pulled from your brain?"

"First," said Annie, "if we look at her behavior, she is obviously conveying something about Leaping and Hopping and there is a Sense of urgency about it. Given the context of our discussion, I'd say that it's for sure that her message is about Transtemporal Leaping. This brings me to what was going on in my mind and my life on Lost and Found Continent when I Heard you Invoking me. You see, Mary, when I listened to you Re-Calling the Hope of Wild Women that the Magnetic field of force can still be conjured among us, I Re-membered what follows in that text (since I mySelf had written and published it in the 2048 BE edition of *Quintessence*). I yelled at you to please stop reading it aloud partly because the sentence that follows carries a strong negative charge. You remember it:

> But harsh experiences of foreground diaspora and fragmentation seemed to be characterized either by the absence of Magnetic attraction or—worse—by aversion, a kind of negative magnetism."[19]

"Yes, I remember it well," I said.

"Obviously, the point is not that either of us is afraid to know or speak about such matters," Annie continued. "Rather, it's a question of strategy."

"Oh, hold on, Annie!" I said loudly. "You know that I believe the best strategy is to Name/Aim Truly and let the chips fall where they may. Tameness is not an acceptable solution."

Annie replied in a strong voice: "Mary, you know that I am no advocate of tameness." Pulling herSelf up, she stood tall, so that she faced me squarely. "You also know that I have studied your writings thoroughly and continue to do so. My loyalty to you and your work is impeccable. There is, however, an Other major factor that I am respectfully asking you to take into account Now." She paused, awaiting my reaction.

I was impressed by Annie's Self-confidence, which was clearly coming from a heightened Sense of Integrity and an inner surge of Elemental Power. I Saw that she Recognized *my* Recognition of these Changes. I caught her Inner Eye, so to speak, just as she caught mine. We both began Be-Laughing. Our waves of Laughter seemed to career around the room and out the window. None of this was lost on Cottie, who was watching us intently, her ears standing high. Then there was stark silence.

It was my turn to speak. "Well, Annie, I understand. That is, *I get it*," I said. "You have been doing some significant Quantum Leaping, yourSelf, and that is somehow related to your disruption of my reading a few minutes ago from your 'Cosmic Comments and Conversations in 2048 BE Concerning Chapter Two.' What was that all about, Annie?"

"It has to do with your association of strategizing with tameness, a quality which we both abhor," replied Annie. "You seemed to be interpreting my decision to eliminate that last sentence as a timid choice to avoid Naming and confrontation with harsh realities such as the absence of Magnetic attraction among women and a kind of aversion among women which I called 'negative magnetism'—realities which admittedly could work to kill off all hope for a Women's Movement."

"Well, you can see that I do not want to eliminate free discussion of such unpleasant realities, even though it is hard to face this stuff," I said.

Annie nodded. "I know what you're saying, Mary. But this is where my Quantum Leaping comes in. The Leaping is not mere avoidance or escapism. It is a kind of *inclusive transcendence*. In fact, it is something like what you have called 'The Third Thing.' Here on Lost and Found we have the advantage of having been freed from many of the crippling effects of physical and mental pollution. So we can Quantum Leap faster, higher, and more effectively, without being stuck in the sort of dead-ended, circular pseudo-arguments that characterized so much academic/academented theorizing that were prevalent in archetypal deadtime."

"Yeah," I replied, "we are all familiar with the type of theorizing that exhausts one's brain and really leads nowhere—for example, much of postmodern gobbledygook."

"So, you understand, Mary, how refreshing it is to breathe fresh air and imbibe more and more Great Vibes both physically and mentally. It makes everything easier and clearer when you are free from an atmosphere that gags you on every level. And the effect is *cumulative.* So Here's the point: The main reason why I stopped you from reading further was that I wanted you to know that I have Leaped Ahead of where I was in 2048 BE, when I wrote that passage. After all, that was seven Biophilic years ago! It's not that I disagree with it exactly, but that my thinking is richer and more complex Now in 2056 BE."

"That's an excellent point, Annie," I said. "I'm thrilled that you've been Leaping ahead. For one thing, I can learn *more* from you. We can have more stimulating conversations. It would be so *boring* if you just stood still. By the way, I've been Leaping ahead also."

We both had a Great Be-Laughing Moment together.

"Annie," I said, "you make me want to Hop over to Lost and Found Right Now." At that second, Cottie Hopped into my arms. "Let's go right away!" I said.

And so we did.

Chapter Fourteen

Back Again:
More on Inclusive Transcendence

My Goodness! That last trip over to Lost and Found was so High and so Fast that Here I am back/ahead again already! I say "back" because I am right at my desk where I was when I took off. I say "ahead" because something has changed inside me. The scope of my vision has widened/heightened/brightened. I say back/ahead because this was a Leap that encompassed Archaic Past and Future dimensions. My Present has expanded.

I just walked into the other room, where Cottie had assumed one of her favorite vibe-sending positions—lying down on her stomach with her tail in my direction. I was not surprised to find that she had shifted positions during my trip. I am not qualified to decode this shift (which may have occurred simply for matters of comfort), but I did notice that she had placed her head instead of her tail in my direction.

Reassuming my place at the desk I looked out and saw that a Stunning sunset was visible there/then, right over the lake outside my window. Awed as always by its breathtaking beauty, I thought of the sight of Brontie on Lost and Found Beach during my last visit. I recalled how extraordinarily Beautiful she was and the Amazing Light that came from her and spread over Lost and Found, gradually engulfing all of us. I also remembered Kate's reflections about her understanding that this Light was actually strengthening our intellects (a work which Thomas Aquinas believed was accomplished by angels).

Brontie continues to shed Light on Quantum Leaping, transcendence, and related realities. Quantum Leaping is not just the exceptional act of an exceptional being. It is massive. It gives rise to critical mass. This not so solitary Leap is inclusive of the slower, apparently more methodical moves of Others that both precede and follow it.

This helps me to understand what has been happening to Annie during the past few Biophilic years. While my contemporaries and I have been slogging onward under that debilitating condition of back there/then (archetypal deadtime), Annie and her companions on Lost and Found have been gaining momentum. They are, more and more, like shooting stars.

So what does this say about my condition and contribution to Realizing the Archaic Future? Does it really mean that I must now move to the back of class? Is it time for us who were/are back there/then to put on dunce caps and humbly sit in the corner of some dilapidated archetypal schoolhouse, waiting to be taught by Annie and her companions as they soar beyond and beyond?

Irritated, I fight off an urge to throw spit balls and mumble "This sucks!"

But wait! This can't be right! Have I regressed totally into patriarchal thinking? Can I imagine only circles? "Have I forgotten my own concept of Spiraling?" I howl. "Am I losing my mind?"

Luckily, the door banged open, just in time. In strode Kate. "What's going on, Mary?" she asked. "What happened between you and Annie?"

"She talked about her Quantum Leaping," I responded. "I don't know why, but I was disoriented by her description of her recent progress. After she left I felt kind of destabilized and lost."

Kate gave me a look of deep sympathy. "Oh, I think I know what you mean. It happened to me, too. I've been trying to understand what actually occurred. You know, Annie has recently experienced enormous energy surges. And remember, since she was *born* on Lost and Found, she is unencumbered by having lived in archetypal deadtime and by being forced to carry those memories. She has been able to Fly, as it were. As her mother I have watched this recent escalation with astonishment. It seems we have engendered a New species on Lost and Found. I think that what you Sensed from her, Mary, is extraordinary Biophilic Power. Since you and I were born in a.d., we have had different histories. But we are also the beneficiaries of this New species of women, who are Realizing the Archaic Future."

"Yes, I See that, Kate," I replied. "So our Powers are also being enhanced as we move on into Realizing the Archaic Future together with Annie and her companions. They are indeed our Foresisters of the Future."

"Yes," said Kate. "And since there has been a temporal sequence, these younger women honor you as a Foresister of the Past, of their Past. They have read your books and are still being formed/informed by them, even as they send you further waves of light so that you can continue to keep on writing."

"So we are rapidly breaking out of patriarchy, with its moldy molds. Together we are overcoming it," I said.

Kate and I looked at each other determinedly, and Cottie sat upright between us. In the middle of this idyllic scene, the door slammed wide open. Sophie stomped in first. Annie and her friend Anowa, Sophie's daughter, stood on the threshold. The great wolf Fenrir, Anowa's Familiar, Nosed her way through and sniffed.

Having learned to take such interruptions in stride, I stepped aside to permit the entry of everyone. It became immediately clear that the mood of the group was solemn ... and urgent.

Glancing quickly at Kate, I saw that she did not appear surprised. As usually happened in the course of such gatherings, everyone adapted to the limited accommodations and found a spot to sit or lie on. Fenrir managed to lie down in the doorway, arranging her rear legs and tail so that they stretched out into the hall.

Sophie was the first to speak. The tall African woman stood proudly. All eyes were riveted on her beautiful face, as she looked around Fiercely at each individual.

"This is a solemn and significant Moment for all of us in this room and for every living being on this planet," she began softly. "Kate asked me to begin this discussion partly because of my identity. As you all know, my Continent of Origin is Africa, the Continent that has suffered most severely from the man-made scourges of the twentieth and twenty-first centuries. I traveled from Africa to America and came Here to Lost and Found with Kate, as an Original member of the Anonyma Network. My daughter, Anowa, was born almost at the same time as Annie, so of course we are like 'family.' And Here we all are! So let's move directly to the subject we need to address right Now."

When Sophie spoke the words "Here we all are!" the scope of her vision stretched beyond those who were then sitting in the room. She was addressing an audience of multitudes of beings Living throughout myriads of Realms of Time and Space. Like Brontie, she emitted a profoundly healing and glorious Light.

Synchronously, the energies in the room shifted. Sophie's voice carried us all into Other dimensions. It was Present in the room; yet it re-sounded far away. It echoed and re-echoed far out in the cosmos, and back again.

Sophie began by passionately calling for Justice. Then she paused rather abruptly and looked around. It appeared that she felt a change in the vibrations among those who were gathered around her. She also Sensed a strong Presence of a Foresister from the Past. "Who is this?" she cried out, looking around. "Who is Here whom I haven't met before?"

"Well, *I* am Here!" announced a strong, clear voice. "My name is Matilda Joslyn Gage."

"Oh, I've heard of you!" exclaimed Sophie. "Your achievements are recorded in the history books that we have in our libraries on Lost and Found Continent. I know that you are a famous Feminist scholar and activist from the nineteenth century in America. And I remember some interesting facts about your home in Fayetteville, New York. I read that anti-slavery meetings were held there and that the house was offered as a station on the Underground Railroad."

"Right you are, Sophie!" said Matilda, who appeared as a white-haired Crone as she approached the tall African woman, while Sophie made her way across the room to greet this distinguished visitor from the Past. There was an air of solemnity and deep E-motion about this Transtemporal meeting.

I glanced out the window and noticed that a crowd of Lost and Found animals and women who showed up for this occasion were beginning to fill the grassy area between my front door and the lake outside. This area appeared to be expanding to accommodate the large gathering. The sense of excitement was palpable. A crowd of Wild geese honked riotously.

Sophie, Matilda, and the rest of us who had been in my crowded apartment poured down the stairs and out the door. We quickly arranged ourselves so that we were seated on the grass, with Sophie and Matilda sitting on two small benches in front of the gathering.

"Well, Sophie," I said, "you were just beginning to speak about Justice, and then Matilda Joslyn Gage surprised us all by her sudden appearance in our midst. I somehow feel that this was no 'mere coincidence.'"

"It was the word *justice* that caught my attention," announced Gage. "When I overheard *that* word I dropped everything, including the speech I was working on, and came running. As you know, Justice has been a subject of passionate concern to me all my life. However, I must confess, Mary, that when I hear you and your contemporaries and Future Foresisters discussing your dilemmas I am frustrated by the limitations of that word. So I am inviting myself in, so to speak, to join the conversation." With a sudden display of shyness, Matilda added: "I mean, if you don't mind, of course."

Sophie tried, and failed, to suppress a laugh. "Well, Matilda," she said, "you can see from the seating arrangements that nobody is put out by your arrival on the scene."

"Quite the contrary," I added from my place on the grass. "We are excited and honored to have you here. It is a startling synchronicity that you are here for the discussion this evening, in the sense that the Timing is perfect. And it is also a Syn-Crone-icity, in accord with the *Wickedary* definition of *Syn-Crone-icities*, which are "'coincidences' experienced and recognized by Crones as Strangely significant."[1]

"You see, Matilda," said Sophie, "it appears that we Crones have all come to a place in our separate quests for justice where we find ourSelves forced to leap beyond justice. The word for what we seek is *Nemesis*."

Reaching for a copy of the *Wickedary*, which "just happened" to be lying in the grass nearby, Sophie turned to the page in Word-Web One of that volume on which *Nemesis* is defined. "Here is the *Wickedary* definition," she said, projecting her voice so that all of the animals and women who were Present could hear:

1: Virtue beyond justice, acquired by Inspired Acts of Righteous Fury; Virtue enabling Seers to unblindfold captive Justice 2: participation in the powers of the Goddess Nemesis; Elemental disruption of the patriarchal balance of terror; Passionate Spinning/Spiraling of Archaic threads of Gynergy."[2]

Sophie added, "According to the *Wickedary*, and to *Webster's* dictionary before it, Nemesis is the Goddess of Divine Retribution. This hurls our imaginations far beyond the limitations of the pedestrian terrain usually associated with discussions of justice."

"I like the Fierce context that is introduced by this way of Naming," said Kate. "For one thing, it brings to the surface the feelings of Fury, or Rage, that we all feel when we think about acts of injustice. It takes away the dispassionate, academic dullness that is associated with discussions of ethics, et cetera. I remember the professors we had in college who droned on and on about 'just war theory.' Yuk!"

Three little ducks who were swimming just offshore in the lake began yukking. Then a number of women began laughing. When this subsided I glanced at Gage's expressive face. She appeared to be having the Time of her life.

"How are you feeling, Matilda?" I ventured.

"Oh, this is just wonderful. I'm feeling right at home!" exclaimed our guest. "I've yearned to unblindfold captive Justice, and here we are, doing it, together! And I do love speaking about Nemesis as the Virtue that is beyond Justice, acquired by 'Inspired Acts of Righteous Fury.' I have very often been Wildly Furious!"

At hearing these words, the entire gathering of Lost and Found animals and women cheered Loudly. There was thumping of tails, by the raccoons especially, Wild flapping of wings by visiting geese, and an assortment of Musical animal sounds. The women, monkeys, and seals clapped. A few women banged on drums.

Anowa jumped up on a tree stump and yelled "Wow!" and then "Whoa!" and finally "Please be quiet so that our guest can speak to us."

Matilda and I then strode over to the center of the grass, and I was carrying *Woman, Church and State*. The cheering and clapping and thumping began again, but it subsided after a few signals from Anowa, Kate, and Sophie.

Turning to Matilda, I asked, "Will you please be so kind, Matilda, as to tell us a bit about how you expressed your Wild Fury back in the nineteenth century?"

"Well, one Elemental cornerstone of my thinking is opposition to touting the 'virtue' of self-sacrifice as evidence of the highest morality."

Turning to our guest, I said, "That is especially clear in your great work *Woman, Church and State*. Will you permit me to read a passage from this book?"

Matilda smiled. "That's fine with me, Mary."

"OK, here goes," I said. Opening the volume to page 316, I read:

> We find those women in whom it [self-sacrifice] has been most apparent have been doing least justice where justice first belongs: to themselves. Justice, as the foundation of the highest law, is a primal requirement of the individual to the self.[3]

"Moreover, you stated:

> But woman is learning for herself that not self-sacrifice but self-development is her first duty in life. And this [is] not primarily for the sake of others, but that she may become fully herself.[4]

"And, Matilda, I would add to this that the exaggeration of self-sacrifice in the conditioning of women is so twisted in its consequences that when we see this, our Natural response is the Rage, or Wild Fury, that can give rise to Nemesis. We recognize such religious brainwashing as a hideous crime against women and we understand more and more deeply the truth of your statement:

> The most stupendous system of organized robbery known has been that of the church towards woman."[5]

Matilda looked pleased. "Mary, I appreciate your acknowledgment of my words. As you know, I have continued always to advocate opposition to the institution which I have identified as 'that most unscrupulous enemy of freedom—the Church.'"[6]

"And, Matilda, it's exciting to recognize that you yourself have become a channel of Nemesis," I exclaimed. "A transformative/Magical/Alchemical Force comes from the depth of your understanding, courage, and love for women. This force manifests your participation in the Goddess Nemesis and is contagious. Would you give us an example of how Contagious Nemesis works?"

"Gladly," responded Gage. "As you are aware, my chief life work, *Woman, Church and State*, was harshly attacked after it first appeared in 1893 by the protestant Anthony Comstock (chief enforcer of the obscenity laws bearing his name), with the cooperation of Thomas W. Sheedy, a prominent catholic, who sat on the school board in my hometown of Fayetteville, New York.

"I had presented a copy of *Woman, Church and State* to the school library. Comstock threatened to arrest the school board members if they placed the book in the school library. My response to the reporter who wished to know the effect of the Comstock-catholic attack upon me illustrates accurately how the Goddess Nemesis works. I said:

> It has acted like a tonic. I have not been well through the summer, not having recovered from over-work on *Woman, Church and State*, but the moment I learned of Comstock's letter and read the falsities so freely printed in regard to my book, I grew better and feel myself able to meet all enemies of whatever name or nature."[7]

"Matilda," I said, "you were exhilarated when catholics and protestants alike began to call for the suppression of your book. You *knew*, didn't you, that the effect of all this public criticism would be to *promote* your great work! You were and still are exuberant."

The audience was mesmerized by our discussion of Gage's work. Everyone wanted the evening to go on and on, and it did. When Matilda made it clear that she wanted to rest, we reluctantly said good-night, but only on the condition that our discussion with her would continue the following afternoon.

CHAPTER FIFTEEN

A LATE-NIGHT
CONVERSATION WITH MATILDA

WHEN I ARRIVED BACK UPSTAIRS IN MY APARTMENT I realized
that I had many questions for Matilda and wondered how I could
contact her. After the convocation she had literally disappeared.
Although we did have a commitment to meet with her the following afternoon, I was impatient at the thought of waiting that
long. Continuing to wonder how I could reach her, I picked up my
copy of *Woman, Church and State*, hoping to find inspiration about
what to do.

Well, that worked like magic! I heard a familiar tap on my door.
Overjoyed, I called out: "Is that Matilda Joslyn Gage?" In an instant she was in the living room. Cottie, who Sensed that she was
a cat lover, ran over to her. I happily followed.

When I saw Matilda, my mood of joy was transformed into
somber intensity, which resonated with the deep Righteous Fury
that I could See in her face and Feel emanating from every cell of
her be-ing—*and my own.*

"I'm so grateful to you for coming here/now," I sputtered. "I've
been studying your great speech *The Dangers of the Hour,* which

you delivered in 1890 at the founding convention of your new women's rights organization—the Woman's National Liberal Union. I was thrilled to picture you standing before the delegates from twenty-seven states who were determined to stop the religious fundamentalists from gaining control of the government. I was deeply moved to learn that these women recognized this as the greatest danger the country faced."

I paused for breath and gazed in awe at my guest, who simply stared at me in silence, as if she expected me to say more. I understood this as a signal to continue: "I know that your speech was absolutely appropriate for the circumstances at the time you wrote it. But, Matilda, *Now is the hour of greatest danger—in the early twenty-first century.*"

"Yes, that's why I came," she replied quietly.

"Right now, at the beginning of the third millennium a.d., religious fundamentalists *are* gaining control of the government!" I paused. Then I added, with a feeling of deep horror, "And they intend to take over the world."

My guest responded quietly: "They must be stopped."

"You saw that danger so clearly in your own time!" I exclaimed. "And you understood so deeply that the major enemy of women is religious fundamentalism—not only as it motivates our oppressors and feeds their fanatic woman-hating habits but also as it weakens and undermines the integrity of the minds and souls of women." I raced on: "And you knew that early childhood religious training was one reason for the slowness of the advance of woman suffrage reform. You realized that fighting only for suffrage was just scratching the surface. As you wrote in *The Liberal Thinker:*

Men trained from infancy by the Church to a belief in woman's inferiority are loath to concede her capable of self-government.[1]

"And of course women have been trained to the same belief by the obsessively hierarchical entity you so accurately Name 'the ecclesiastical machine.' Will you permit me to read a brief passage you wrote about this 'machine'?"

"Mary," she said, trying to speak patiently, "I know what it says! I wrote it. Remember? I'm dying to hear more from *you* about the dangers of *this* hour!"

"Right you are, Matilda," I said. "Maybe I was unconsciously avoiding talking about it. You see, I've been in a state of horror thinking about this, and it's very comforting to speak to you about *your* time."

My guest flinched. "It was not so comfortable for *me* then, Mary. Some of my closest friends and allies in the National Woman Suffrage Association had turned against me and abandoned me. I already Sensed that there was a plot afoot to write me out of the history of the Woman Suffrage Movement. And, as I stated in *The Liberal Thinker*, 'the woman suffrage reform advances slowly.' I pointed out that 'newcomers [among woman suffrage societies] and many of the old ones fear to take an advance step, and from motives of business or social policy, cater to their worst enemy, the Church.'"

"Yes, you did write about all those things very admirably," I said. "You very clearly Named the context of this regression of women. I recall how you described the nation's crisis at that time, coming from the encroachments of 'the Christian Party in Politics,' which was composed of both catholics and protestants and which aimed to bring about a union of Church and State. And Matilda, I have a copy of your publication *The Liberal Thinker* right here on my desk. Will you do me the honor of reading this great paragraph? Here!"

Matilda picked up the document I had emphatically placed before her and read out loud the lines I had marked:

Therefore not alone to aid her own enfranchisement—valueless without religious liberty—but in order to help preserve the very life of the Republic, it is imperative that women should unite upon a platform of opposition to the teaching and aim of that ever most unscrupulous enemy of freedom—the Church.[2]

"Thank you, Bold Foresister," I said. "And now, forgive me for reading one more sentence from *The Liberal Thinker:* 'Let Church and State forever remain separate.'³ Recently some of the news media have taken on this issue, exposing the antics of the religious right in their crusade to spread the belief that the American tradition is firmly on the side of union of church and state."⁴

Matilda then faced me squarely. "So it is Time Now for us to really make bold and face *the dangers of this hour.*"

"I've been thinking about where to begin," I said. "First, I want to tell you that I am deeply sorry and ashamed that the united states of america is failing so badly to live up to your hopes and expectations. Despite your brilliance and courage, your tireless efforts and great successes, this country is now a nightmare, and it is spreading its horror around the globe. This is not good news for you, but I am hoping we can communicate about it. We need your historical perspective."

My guest was deeply affected by these words. She spoke slowly: "Mary, I want you to understand my situation as distinct from that of your friends, the Future Foresisters who live in the Archaic Future. You see, I have made a conscious decision to remain in the past—at least for the Moment—precisely because you do need my historical perspective. In order to be of help, I need to stay when and where I have lived and acted, I need to 'stand my ground,' so to speak. From this etheric dimension I can understand what you tell me of your time, and hopefully I can draw from my own experience to help shed light on your situation so you can figure out what to do."

"That's as much as I could possibly ask, Matilda," I replied gratefully. "Brava!"

"Now, then, let's get on with it!" she said. "You were saying that our country is now a nightmarish place. Will you elaborate? As you know, I am able to 'tune in' from this dimension, but I cannot know all of the details."

"OK," I said. "Let me start with the forty-third US President, George W. Bush, and his use of religion. It has been noticeable for some time that this nonelected president is an ultraconservative christian who believes that god has called him to be president and whose core constituency is the religious right. He and his cronies are waging the worst assault on separation of church and state in the history of our country. Taxpayer money has been doled out to favored churches in his 'faith-based initiative.' This and his other actions, such as the appointment of judges who could be counted on to tear down the wall that separates church and state and his insane insistence that his pre-emptive war against Iraq was justified and successful, are legitimated by this born-again Führer who bestows 'god's approval' on the whole horror show."

"This is all very reminiscent of fundamentalist strategies in my time," commented Matilda. "I am sure that Bush's agenda must include woman-hating at its core. Am I right?"

"You are absolutely right on, Matilda," I said. "These evils are all interconnected. They are all parts of the same 'package,' which is promoted by what I like to call the 'gruesome twosome' of the religious right, Pat Robertson and Jerry Falwell. These men and their ilk were deftly exposed some time ago by the great television journalist Walter Cronkite, who pointed out that both Robertson and Falwell called a terrorist attack against this country 'God's punishment' against feminists and other groups they despise."[5] I paused when I noticed the questioning expression on Matilda's face.

"Obviously your allusions to historical events beyond my time cannot fit within my frame of reference, but I can surmise what you are talking about," she said. "If you feel that too many detailed explanations would sidetrack our conversation, I accept your judgment on that."

"Oh, OK," I said, grateful to be relieved of the phenomenal task of trying to explain too much about the changes that have occurred during more than one hundred years that separate our lifetimes. "Matilda is cool," I thought. "She understands." I decided to postpone discussion of technological, social, and linguistic changes that I knew my guest would be intensely curious about. So I bumbled along.

"One of the most disturbing things about Bush is his use of religious language to communicate with his evangelical followers. His speeches are laced with religious code words—a fact that is not always noticed by secular audiences. These specially charged words are intended to be heard on one level by the general public and on another level by his devoted core audience. For example, in Bush's Republican National Convention speech in August 2004, he used the phrase 'I believe' innumerable times.

"I was not surprised, then, to hear Bush, in the first televised presidential debate with John Kerry on September 30, 2004, repeatedly and emphatically using this expression—thereby signaling his right-wing constituents about his own religiosity. But then I noticed something startling: Kerry began repeatedly using the same phrase to preface his own quite different 'beliefs.' When Kerry used it, his voice was very strong and 'presidential.' I am convinced that Kerry's choice was no accident. I think that he and/or his handlers consciously planned this choice of words. It would seem that such a choice would be baffling to Bush and others. Indeed, Bush looked shaken by Kerry's power and intelligence. Perhaps he had not anticipated the possibility that Kerry would parrot his words so effectively to convey a different message."

When I finally paused and looked at Matilda, she appeared to be both puzzled and intrigued. "Mary," she said earnestly, "I am not able to contain my curiosity any longer about the word *televised.* What do you mean when you describe the presidential debate as 'televised'?"

"Oh, I apologize, Matilda," I said, with genuine remorse. "I guess I was so eager to rush ahead with the ideas that I have been unintentionally rude. I'm sorry. Please come on over to the next room. I want to show you something."

I led my guest into the room I call my "office" and pointed to the TV. "That's my 'television set,'" I announced.

Gage seemed quite unimpressed. "Well, it seems to be a brown box with a window in its front—and some knobs. Oh, and there are some things like ropes hanging down in the back. Perhaps I should turn a knob," she said, reaching over to touch the set.

"Oh, Matilda!" I said loudly, fearing that she would be alarmed at the sounds and moving pictures. "Please don't touch it yet." I dragged two chairs across the room and placed them in front of the TV. Inviting her to sit down, I added awkwardly, "Here are a couple of chairs. I think I should first give you a brief introductory explanation."

My visitor smiled tolerantly at what seemed to her to be extreme caution on my part, but she seated herself politely. I switched on the remote control, which was adjusted to a higher volume than I had intended. Suddenly the TV blasted forth violent explosive noises—bombs, shots, and sirens—accompanied by vivid colored images of moving tanks and planes and burning buildings and of people dying in pools of blood on the streets. On the screen were printed the words "The Bombing of Baghdad." It was about the infamous event that happened in 2002 when Bush waged his pre-emptive war on Iraq. Matilda jumped up and appeared to be searching desperately for a hiding place.

"Oh, please excuse this!" I said, putting a hand on her arm in what I hoped would be a soothing gesture. Then I felt an absence. My guest had left.

I made myself a cup of coffee—which I then spilled—and fretted. After what seemed like an eternal pause I heard a loud knock on my door. "Come in," I called anxiously. She did. For a Moment we just stood and stared at each other.

"It's an astonishing thing," she said. "We seem to be able to bridge the gap that separates us despite all these changes. And we are not abandoning the effort, are we?"

"Certainly not," I said.

"Now, about what we saw together on television," Matilda began. "It is obvious that television is a very powerful medium, but clearly there is a problem about who controls it. In the scenes we just saw, a cruel and savage attack was launched by a supremely powerful rich Western nation against a small, poverty-stricken

"You know, Mary, there is something depressingly familiar about all of this," said my visitor. "In my time, women had to confront the same demons. The ecclesiastical machine worked in the same way. But in your time it is reinforced by such monstrous technological media."

"Then we have to Spiral around again to face the problem of sameness and the illusion of progress," I said.

"So, let's move on!" Gage exclaimed urgently.

CHAPTER SIXTEEN

FOCUSING ON THE PRESENT TOGETHER

GAGE BEGAN THE CONVERSATION. "Mary, I have a strong Sense that it is urgently necessary for us to focus on what is happening right at this very Moment. I can feel that there is an enormous conflict swirling all around you. This is an extraordinary time in patriarchal history, isn't it?"

"You know it is, Matilda!" I answered. "An emerging cognitive minority of women are convinced that we are witnessing and experiencing the death throes of patriarchy, which has been around for only about five thousand years. After all, women exercised great power for many thousands of years before that. I have inelegantly remarked upon occasion that as far as longevity is concerned, patriarchy has been a mere squirt of sperm. Within that moribund system, over that time, males have killed and massively destroyed women and other life forms. It is high time for that system to self-destruct and for Biophilic be-ing to re-emerge."

"Well spoken!" declared my guest in a hearty tone. Cottie danced and leaped across the room in celebration of Free Felinity.

"Fine! She's saying that the animals are with us," I said. "My proposal for how we can proceed with this discussion is to confront the foreground events of each day as they occur. You have inspired this plan with your comment that this is an extraordinary time and that it is urgently necessary to focus on what is happening right at this very Moment. Shortly after you made that comment I went downstairs and picked up the recently delivered *New York Times* for October 12, 2004. The headline that first caught my eye on page 1 shouted: 'Group of Bishops Using Influence to Oppose Kerry.'[1] I immediately thought, 'This is one for Matilda!'"

I handed the paper to Gage and asked her to read it. She looked very attentive. "Interesting!" she exclaimed quietly as she read the paper. "That is exactly what they would do." Then she added with a scowl, "They are still exactly *the same.*" We both laughed in exasperation.

"But it is not really amusing," I said. "It gave me the chills when I read it," I added with a shudder. "I have read some of your comments about ecclesiastical tricks, and I know how aware you always were of the dishonest behavior of clergy, both catholic and protestant, in their continual slimy efforts to keep women down."

Despite her effort to maintain self-control, my visitor suddenly waved the newspaper at me and said in an angry voice: "Aha! After the unsavory headline which you just read, there follows a shorter heading announcing that abortion is the 'key issue.' Then comes yet another heading to the same article: 'But Prelates Take Pains to Avoid Overt Backing of Bush's Campaign.'"

"Yes, it is disgusting, Matilda," I said. "See, *The New York Times* did a good job of laying it out for the reader. The first paragraph sets the scene:

> For Archbishop Charles J. Chaput, the highest ranking Roman Catholic prelate in Colorado, a swing state, there is only one way for a faithful Catholic to vote in this presidential election, for President Bush and against Senator John Kerry.[2]

"The article goes on to reveal Archbishop Chaput's strategy. Its authors report that in his address to a group of catholic college students the prelate 'stopped short of telling them whom to vote for, but he reminded them of Mr. Kerry's support for abortion rights.'"

"Oh, that is *so* disgusting!" exclaimed Matilda. "He's manipulating the minds of young people so that they will vote for the most dangerous, woman-hating, life-hating imbecile imaginable, allowing him to continue destroying the country and the world as President of the United States."

"Yes, it is an indescribably horrible prospect," I said. "And Chaput is not alone. He belongs to a group of catholic bishops who are fanatically intent upon throwing the weight of the church into the elections, and who identify abortion as a nonnegotiable issue (together with a few other issues like gay marriage and embryonic stem cell research). One of the most hideous parts of Chaput's program is his insistence that to vote for Kerry would be a *sin* that must be *confessed* before receiving communion. The reason: because a vote for Kerry would be 'cooperating in evil.'"

Gage was visibly horrified. "So this is the ecclesiastical machine in one of its most virulent manifestations. And to think I believed that in the nineteenth century the United States was at a low stage of progress!"

"But you and your followers were not at all at a low stage, Matilda," I insisted. "Quite the opposite! Let me read your own words from *The Liberal Thinker:*

> The "ecclesiastical machine" through the ages has taught the existence of a superior and an inferior class of mankind; the superior being the priesthood, as mediator between God and man. The inferior, the laity, again sub-divided into the superior male, the inferior female. Mrs. Alice Scatcherd of England writes that she now dares to publicly say that the Church teaches men submission; women *abject* submission.[3]

"I really love that last statement by Mrs. Alice Scatcherd," I said. "She must have been just one of your many readers who were stirred by you to speak bravely and develop their own thoughts.

You were and still are so alive with Contagious Courage that you generated a morphic resonance among women. You stimulated them with the electric current of your own Gynergy. That is, you *galvanized* them into Feminist Daring, Matilda. That's why we need your Encouraging Presence with us Now!"

Gage, who had been listening intently, sat up very straight in the hard, wooden chair. "And you *do* have me!" she responded Fiercely. "Surely you can understand in your own twenty-first-century context the statement that I published in 1880 in *National Citizen and Ballot Box,* a newspaper that I founded and edited. I then wrote:

> The women of to-day are the thoughts of their mothers and grandmothers, embodied and made alive. They are active, capable, determined and bound to win. They have a thousand generations back of them. The pressure lies not alone in their own veins and arteries, but the hereditary transmission of qualities is making itself felt. Millions of women, dead and gone, are speaking through us to-day. If we are false to woman's demands, we are false to the mothers who bore us. The revenge of time lies in our hands."[4]

"That passage has always given me the chills, Matilda," I said, almost in a whisper. "You were writing in 1880 of 'the women of today.' And now, in the desperate 'today' of the first decade of the twenty-first century, you are saying these words again—hoping, I guess, that we will finally get your message. May those millions of women speak to us and through us again . . . Today!"

"I think I hear them saying, 'Get back to work!'" said my guest with a purposeful look. "So now, let's get on with our analysis of the nasty business stirred up by the jesuitical clergy serving the goals of the bushites."

"I like the way you say the word *jesuitical,*" I exclaimed with a laugh. "According to *Webster's* dictionary, *Jesuit* means 'a member of the Roman Catholic Society of Jesus founded by Ignatius Loyola in 1534 and devoted to missionary and educational work.' As you undoubtedly know, the adjective derived from this is defined as 'given to intrigue or equivocation.'"

"Yes, that's exactly what I had in mind," responded my honored guest. "And the word can apply to protestants as well as catholics of that ilk. It was commonly used in my day."

"And it continues to be used in mine," I said.

"It's still *the same*," we said together, as we burst out laughing.

I snatched up the newspaper with distaste. "Just listen to this: The authors of the *Times* article point out that 'the Bush campaign has spent four years cultivating Catholic leaders, organizing more than 50,000 volunteers and hiring a corps of paid staff members to increase Catholic turnout.' What do you think about this, Matilda?" I asked.

"Well, Mary, as we both know very well, this is mere opportunism on both sides. Obviously, the Bush people want to court the catholics, but only because of their numbers and organized power. As I wrote in *The Dangers of the Hour:*

> The Protestant pulpit is only less dangerous than the Catholic to the liberties of the people in that its organized strength is less."[5]

"Yes, we are agreed on that," I said. "And I know that you realize that the bullying, manipulative maneuvers of an Archbishop Chaput in his attempts to intimidate catholics into believing that to vote for Kerry is a sin are not essentially different from the bullying of church-goers by protestant clergy. You have explained clearly that 'it is imperative that women should unite on a platform of opposition to the teachings and aim of that ever most unscrupulous enemy of freedom—the Church.' And the word *Church* includes all of its branches."[6]

I continued: "Now, Matilda, I would like to move on to the subject of the apparently Momentous importance of the vote in America at this time, especially as we approach Election Day, which is November 2, 2004. This is a hair-raising time in the history of the United States. There is a feeling among many that anything can happen. A significant number view Bush not only as stupid, but as a maniac, fascist, 'born-again' fanatic who thinks that he has a direct line to 'God.' The problem is that he has a lot of support. Apparently there are thousands, indeed millions, who blindly believe him, follow him, and will vote for him. There is reason to think that he will stop at nothing in order to stay in power. Some believe that he might even start World War III (there already were two world wars in the twentieth century) in order to distract the populace and maintain his stranglehold. The dangers of *this* hour are intensified by the fact that the presidential race is razor close, while at the same time there are serious problems with the voting procedures and equipment. So the election could be chaotic. Suspense is widespread and intense."

"And I suppose the role of the media is largely obfuscation?" Gage queried.

"That's correct," I responded. "With the notable but tenuous exception of public broadcasting, the airwaves are loaded with obfuscation, since the commercial television networks and radio stations are for the most part corporate owned. Of course, this applies also to the print media, including newspapers and magazines."

"I am interested in the role of corporations," said Gage. "As you know, their rise to power dominated the last decades of the nineteenth century."

I jumped in: "I am eager to hear more from you about the history of corporations, Matilda, but first I think we need to understand each other better about the importance of woman suffrage. I know that you worked valiantly for the cause of suffrage. You never abandoned that cause, but in some important ways you outgrew it, isn't that true?"

"Well, you are right, Mary," said Gage. "I've never been a 'one-idea person.' And I learned from experience that many of my suffragist contemporaries were limited by the weakness of having one-track minds."

"I greatly respect the power of your mind to search deeply into things and to reach out and seek to understand the many events and circumstances that must be taken into consideration when we are making important decisions," I said. "In her Introduction to the 1994 reprint of your speech *The Dangers of the Hour* (first delivered on February 24, 1890), Sally Roesch Wagner quotes you as saying:

> I am still a suffragist, but I am more than a suffragist. I have found the old garment useless and have put on a new robe. The slow growth of this movement I have made my study, and at last have been convinced that the stumbling blocks to woman's political enfranchisement can only be rolled away by her mental and spiritual liberation.[7]

"You saw then that the greatest danger this country faced was religious fundamentalists gaining control of the government. And you saw that religious fundamentalism is the major enemy of women, didn't you, Matilda?" I plunged on. "You know, it horrifies me to realize that we have now come around to a point in American history when that enemy threatens even more forcefully to take over. What good does it do for women to have the right to vote if their mental and spiritual powers are eroded by fundamentalist brainwashing? There is an uncanny synchronicity involved here. Just a few days ago I was reading the results of a poll, indicating that 42 percent of American citizens claim be evangelical christians. I'm beginning to feel surrounded by born-agains! Talk about 'one-track minds'!"

"You have reason to be frightened, Mary. When I spoke at that first convention of the Woman's National Liberal Union I admitted publicly that I was frightened at the erosion of freedom happening at the hands of the religious right."

"And there is even more reason to fear such erosion if Bush's 'faith-based government' is allowed to stand," I said. Then I stopped and turned directly to my visitor. "Matilda, I am in a shocked, vertiginous state of mind, because a number of realizations have come to me and converged rather quickly in late October 2004. I would like to talk these over with you and get your 'take' on them. I respect your great courage, your intelligence and insight, and your faithfulness to the cause of women and nature. The urgency of this hour drives me to this very direct mode of communication. Are you still with me?"

The look on my visitor's face was impatient and intense. "Let's get on with it," she said.

"Right!" I said. "I'll begin with a description of George W. Bush's crimes against nature. In a talk he gave in October 2004, Robert F. Kennedy Jr. spoke about the 'excess of corporate power and [its] corrosive impact... on our democracy.' In that context he has written about the 'stealth attack' by the Bush administration on the environment, which is part of a 'concerted deliberate attempt to eviscerate 30 years of environmental law.'[8]

"Matilda, the constant rhetoric the bushites use to conceal their destructive agenda is a device which I call *reversal* and which the famous dystopian novelist and social critic George Orwell called *doublespeak*. Kennedy shows how this mechanism works to hide the destruction of the environment:

> When they destroy the forest, they call it the Healthy Forest Law; when they destroy the air they call it the Clear Skies Bill. And most insidiously they have put polluters in charge of virtually all the agencies that are supposed to protect Americans from pollution. The head of the Forest Service is a timber industry lobbyist. The head of public lands is a mining industry lobbyist who believes that public lands are unconstitutional. The head of the air division at EPA [Environmental Protection Agency] is a utility lobbyist who has represented the worst air polluters in America.[9]

"And so it goes on and on. The point is that the polluters are running/ruining regulatory agencies that are supposed to regulate *them*."

When I paused to catch my breath, I heard Matilda's beseeching voice. "Please stop!" she said.

"OK," I said.

"What do you mean by the word *lobbyist*, pray tell?" she asked.

"Oh!" I responded. "A lobbyist is one who seeks to influence legislators in favor of some special interest. Why didn't you stop me if you didn't understand?"

She stared at me in disbelief. Then she replied patiently: "How could I stop a speeding railroad train?"

"I see," I said, with some embarrassment.

Matilda continued: "Never mind. I think I have a general comprehension of what you are attempting to communicate. I think you are saying that these lobbyists and indeed the whole system of discourse and behavioral interaction are infested and legitimized with 'reversal' and 'doublespeak.' You are saying that these lobbyists and those they represent are subverting the very laws they claim to be enforcing, right?"

"Right, Matilda," I said. "And 'those they represent' are corporations that control our government and steal what belongs to the people, including our air and water and public lands. They are creating what Robert F. Kennedy Jr. calls 'a science fiction nightmare,' in which 'the air is too poisonous to breathe' and the waterways are becoming filthier."[10]

"And I suppose these corporations have extended their tentacles almost everywhere in America," said Gage in tones of shock and anger.

"And around the world," I added.

"Yes, of course!" agreed my friend. "I'm beginning to understand more about the extent of it."

"It's important to understand that the Bush administration is supported by funding from corrupt corporations. Bush and his very rich cronies have wreaked havoc on America and the world. Bush has destroyed the environment, greatly damaged women, the poor, the elderly, and racial and ethnic minorities. He grabs more and more from the poor and dispossessed, giving everything to the wealthy and privileged. His unjustified and hideously cruel war on Iraq has not reached any conclusion. There is a dreadful mess in that suffering country that only continues to get worse. The massive slaughter and maiming continue unabated. The war has served as a propaganda victory for terrorists, giving them ever greater reason for hatred of America."

Gage listened attentively. "So," she said in an enraged voice, "you are saying that this wretched fool has spread suffering and confusion and dishonored America beyond belief."

I groaned, "Oh, Matilda, Americans are now hated and despised all over Europe and, in fact, all over the world."

"But that would seem to be unfair," Matilda started to object.

I said: "But America has prided itself on being a democracy. We have the universal suffrage *you* fought for! It is believed that the people elected Bush! It is not understood by most people that the republicans *stole* the 2000 election. And even for those who grasp the fact that this was a stolen election, there is much about this problem that remains murky. Some Europeans, for example, ask why, in this very democratic country, this mistake can't be corrected. They say, 'You can organize, you can have protests, *you can vote!*'"

Gage pounded the table in frustration and pent-up fury. "There was no possibility of moving fast enough, was there?" she asked.

"It was like one of those nightmares in which you try to run, but your feet are frozen, you try to scream but your voice doesn't work," I said. "In a word, people were bamboozled by the countless lies and reversals that had been hurled at us for four years by Bush and his cartoonlike array of cronies. And there was not only the arrogant lying. There also was the hideous secrecy that was masking unspeakable failure and incompetence on the part of our 'leaders.'"

Gage abruptly stood up and began pacing. She spoke harshly. "There has to be something else that can help explain this strange phenomenon of passivity," she muttered.

"I've been thinking about it constantly," I said. "When I have spoken about it to my friends, they've told me that they also think about it all the time. And they are all anti-Bush and anti-war."

"I believe that is true," Gage said grimly. "From what you are telling me, it seems to me that you are caught in a poisonous atmosphere that is causing spiritual paralysis."